MORE
THAN
BOOTY

Books by Jane
and Barney Crile

TREASURE DIVING HOLIDAYS

MORE THAN BOOTY

MORE
THAN
BOOTY

Jane and
Barney Crile

McGraw-Hill Book Company
New York   Toronto   London

To the memory of
JANE CRILE
Who wrote part of this book
And inspired all of it

—Barney Crile

CONTENTS

Contents

viii

PROLOGUE

*There is no remembrance of former things;
neither shall there be any remembrance of
things that are to come with those that shall
come after.*

Ecclesiastes 1:11

As a surgeon I have dealt for thirty years with
the satisfactions of seeing lives prolonged and with the
sadnesses of watching premature deaths. In this time I
have known patients who were devoutly religious, in
the conventional sense of the word, yet who were so
terrified of death, and perhaps of their thoughts of an
afterworld, that they could not enjoy their remaining
span of life. It has seemed to me that now there are
more of such people than there were a generation ago.
This may be due to the impact of science on religion.

In both man and animals, fear of death is instinctive, for it is necessary for the preservation of life. But animals do not project their personalities into an afterworld. They fear death-dealing agents, but not the concept of death. They are not haunted by morbid fears. Voltaire once said, "I envy the beasts two things—their ignorance of evil to come, and their ignorance of what is said about them."

Long before either Jane or I were brushed by thoughts of death, we were amateur naturalists and we introduced into the back yard of our house a stream of animal life that we watched ebbing and flowing from season to season, bringing births and deaths in their perpetual repetitions. From these experiences, from impressions gained on trips in the wilderness, in the course of diving for treasure on lonely reefs, from adventures in underwater archeology, from friends who came from ancient oriental cultures and from travels in foreign lands, we developed what might be termed a naturalistic philosophy. This philosophy was basically a Darwinian philosophy, for its roots were embedded in the necessity of adapting to change.

In a naturalistic philosophy, as in the ancient, animalistic cult of Pan, there is respect for all of nature. There is no recognition of absolute good or absolute evil. The wolf is no worse than the lamb. In this philosophy there is no concept of truth except as the most accurate interpretation that at the moment we are able to make of the things we see about us.

Because both Jane and I represented the second generation of families that had had naturalistic beliefs, and because we had accepted them early in life, we had time to test this philosophy on ourselves—in our childhoods, in full maturity, in the births of our children and in the deaths of those whom we cherished the most. We believed that death was as much a part of life as birth is, that the two must be accepted alike, and that excessive fear of death may result in lives devoted uselessly to death's propitiation. In this philosophy, as in the cult of Pan, nature became semidivine, the earth and its inhabitants were respected because through the eons they had changed and evolved and adapted and each had taken its proper place in the history of evolution.

Carl Sandburg said of Lincoln "He could ask himself about what is called 'good' and what is called 'bad' and how they are criss-crossed in the human mesh." If children could be raised with this understanding of good and bad perhaps they would have a better comprehension of the world they live in. It might then be possible to recapture some of the sense of beauty and divinity that the ancients felt about the world in the days of Pan.

So might I, standing on this pleasant lea,
Have glimpses that would make me less forlorn;
Have sight of Proteus rising from the sea,
And hear old Triton blow his wreathed horn.
                                        —Wordsworth

We had traveled far and wide in the lands under the sun until coming home satisfied us more than booty.

—The Koran

MORE
THAN
BOOTY

1

ONE KIND
OF LOVE—
CLEVELAND, 1962

The wolf also shall dwell with the lamb,
And the leopard shall lie down with the kid;
And the calf and the young lion and the fatling
together;
And a little child shall lead them . . .
They shall not hurt nor destroy
In all my holy mountain.

The Bible—The Vision of Isaiah

Jane and I always were interested in everything living. Both of us had been brought up in close touch with nature. Every summer during Jane's childhood, a schoolteacher and naturalist, Maud Doolittle, came to spend a few weeks. Jane and her sisters and Miss Doolittle would wander together in the woods where the children learned the names of the ferns and flowers and trees, and to recognize the birds and their particular songs. And every Sunday, her father would take Jane horseback riding in the woods; they went even in the rain or snow. "It's only the things you *don't* do that you regret," he told her, and she never forgot.

As a boy I had spent summertimes in the country, too, and raised animals and worked in my father's laboratory. He was one of the leading biological philosophers of his time, as well as being a surgeon. He encouraged my leanings toward the world of nature.

Jane and I grew up in the same community in Cleveland, and when we were in our early teens, we rode, swam, and played tennis together. In the long years of our courtship, we spent most of our time outdoors. We had the same strong love for it. Our tastes were so similar that, as I look back to the time of our marriage, it was as though we had always been together. In a sense we had, because our association dated from childhood and from the beginnings of our memories.

Life for us in the early days of our marriage was busy. I was deeply engaged in the practice of surgery and in clinical research and medical writing. Jane was fully occupied with the babies, the home, and her hobby of photography. Weekends, when we could get away, we went to the country to ride or to hunt, fish, swim, or search for Indian relics or just to camp with the children at "The Knob," a hilly, unspoiled forest that was then the property of my father.

Our house was in a suburb, Cleveland Heights. Jane and I had been married for three years when we moved into this home. Ann was two, and Joan just born. We fenced the yard about a hundred feet square, to contain them and Susie and George who followed. The yard was their playpen.

One day we dug a pit to cook a young pig for an Hawaiian feast, a *luau*. The pig was wrapped in green cornhusks and buried with hot rocks so that the steam from the husks cooked it slowly all day long. When we dug it up its fat had melted away and it was soft and tender. The day after the *luau* it rained and the hole filled up with water. Jane looked at the puddle. "It's a duck pond," she said. I agreed, for it was easier to make a duck pond than to fill in the hole and put back the sod.

We had the pit made bigger, cemented and lined with stones. The little stream that fed the pond was supplied by a recirculating pump and ran over tiny boulders, making miniature rapids and a waterfall too. Ducklings floated on the placid surface of the pond. The garden never was planned, it simply evolved, and gradually filled with life and warmth and interest. As it grew it developed a Japanese look with the mossy, stone-lined pool, the little waterfall, a wooden bridge over the running stream, dwarf pine trees, a tea house, and great stones scattered here and there in the myrtle and grass. It was in this back yard that we kept wood ducks and mallards, a Canada goose, a swan, two golden pheasants, a cocker spaniel, a chicken, a pet pigeon, a rabbit, and once a baby deer—all of them uncaged. Nature, in an inexhaustible stream of life, moved in, and gave us insight into the factors that shape the lives of animals and possibly also those of man. As we observed the ways of the animals it seemed to us that Audubon had been right when, long ago, commenting on a talk before the Natural History Society of London, he wrote:

> *Captain Hall expressed some doubts as to my views respecting the affection and love of pigeons, as if I made it human, and raised the possessors quite above the brutes. I presume the love of the (pigeon) mothers for their young is much the same as the love of a woman for her offspring. There is but one kind of love: God is love, and all his creatures derive theirs from his; only it is modified by the different degrees of intelligence in different beings and creatures.*

And we found that the strongest single factor in the creation of the love to which Audubon referred was the phenomenon of imprintation.

When a goose is separated from its kind and raised by hand right from the egg, its reactions to people become almost human. This is the principle of *imprintation**—the baby's acceptance, as its mother, of whatever creature it happens to be with during the critical period at which imprintation takes place.

Imprintation occurs in almost every animal that requires the care of a parent. The classical example is "Mary's lamb," an orphan, no doubt, that Mary had raised on a bottle so that "everywhere that Mary went the lamb was sure to go."

Darwin, in *The Voyage of the Beagle,* describes a classical example of imprintation in the way in which the sheep dogs were trained in Banda Oriental, South America:

---

* Konrad Z. Lorenz, *King Solomon's Ring.*

While staying at this estancia, I was amused with what I saw and heard of the shepherd-dogs of the country. When riding, it is a common thing to meet a large flock of sheep guarded by one or two dogs, at the distance of some miles from any house or man. I often wondered how so firm a friendship had been established. The method of education consists in separating the puppy, while very young, from the bitch, and in accustoming it to its future companions. An ewe is held three or four times a day for the little thing to suck, and a nest of wool is made for it in the sheep-pen; at no time is it allowed to associate with other dogs, or with the children of the family. The puppy is, moreover, generally castrated; so that, when grown up, it can scarcely have any feelings in common with the rest of its kind. From this education it has no wish to leave the flock, and just as another dog will defend his master, man, so will these the sheep. It is amusing to observe, when approaching a flock, how the dog immediately advances barking, and the sheep all close in his rear, as if round the oldest ram. These dogs are also easily taught to bring home the flock, at a certain hour in the evening. Their most troublesome fault, when young, is their desire of playing with the sheep for in their sport they sometimes gallop their poor subjects most unmercifully.

Baby birds and most baby mammals are dependent on their mothers and are imprintable. Creatures like turtles or alligators whose eggs are hatched by the sun and whose young must fend for themselves cannot be imprinted.

The time at which imprintation takes place differs with different animals, but it always coincides with the period in which the animal is first able to escape from an enemy. Since baby chickens, ducks, geese, and lambs can follow their mothers and escape as soon as they are born, it is in the first twenty-four hours that imprintation is most effective. We found that chicks forty-eight hours or more old could still be imprinted, but if they were left with the hen for longer than a week, the acceptance of another creature would rarely be strong or persistent. In animals like dogs and coons that are born blind and helpless it always seemed to us that it was not until the baby was able to move around and escape that it was imprintable. Foxes and wolves are said to be the same.

The period of imprintation of pigeons and other birds born helpless coincides with the time just before the bird learns to fly. We separated a baby pigeon from its mother and hand-fed it until it acted as though we were its mother. After it grew up, it flew into the kitchen to roost each night. Every morning we opened the door and it flew outdoors.

Gozzle was a wild Canada goose's egg when we first saw her. We took charge of her destiny as soon as she was hatched. Her mother and father were mildly imprinted Canada geese that in full flight would set their wings and come down at their owner's call. But these geese had been picked up when they were several days old and were never imprinted as firmly as Gozzle was.

Gozzle became a little ball of fuzz that sat in our hands or followed peeping behind us wherever we went. For four days she cried so miserably when she was left alone that we put a recently hatched mallard in the box with her. This satisfied the duckling because it was still in the imprintable stage, but the gosling could be satisfied with nothing less than a person, preferably our daughter, Susie, who had tended her from the first.

Since the duckling took so well to the goose, we put a two-day-old chick in with the duck and then put the three babies together again. The chicken was imprinted on the duck and the duck on the goose. Susie led the parade; the goose followed her, the duck followed the goose, and the chicken the duck. For over a month this ill-assorted brood trooped through our back yard, ignoring the other birds and the dog, each intent on keeping close to its adopted parent.

The imprintations of the chicken and the duck were incomplete because they had not been put together, like the goose and Susie, from the instant of hatching. Gozzle's imprintation never left her. When Susie ran across the lawn, Gozzle, who had become a full-grown Canada goose, flew after her, honking. When anyone sat outside in a chair, Gozzle always went to work on his shoelaces, trying to eat them like worms. Often when I was reading or writing, Gozzle sat beside me, for hours, gabbling amiably in soft tones. When there were troubles or problems I could not solve, I would go to the garden and discuss the matter with Gozzle; she never gave me bad advice.

The early experiences of a bird or mammal may have a profound effect on its adult sexual behavior. Experiments with monkeys have shown that a baby monkey reared alone and fed by a mechanical imitation of a monkey mother never makes a satisfactory sexual adjustment in later life. In order to develop normally it has to have either a true monkey mother to care for it or, if reared on a mechanical mother, it has to have monkey children to play with from an early stage.

Normally wood ducks do not attempt to mate with mallards, but if a wood duck egg is placed under a mallard hen, and the wood duckling is raised with mallard ducklings, when it matures it may prefer to mate with mallards. If a turkey gobbler is raised to sexual maturity without birds of its kind, it may seek for a mate a symbol of the person on whom it is imprinted, such as a shoe. It may try to copulate with this, disregarding a nearby turkey hen.

Although Gozzle's imprintation never wore off, the mallard duck finally separated from the goose and went its way. It never mingled with the other mallards, though, and it led a lonely life, one of the tragedies of imprintation.

We watched the chicken to see if she, like the duck, would be doomed to loneliness, for there were no other chickens in our back yard. Although a hen, she laid no eggs for over a year, and did not associate with the ducks or pheasants. Then we let a young male rabbit loose in the yard.

He had been raised from a baby by our daughter, Joan. She had taken him with her to Boston where she was studying at Radcliffe for an M.A.T. in biology, and he had attended a number of classes, stuffed into her large pocketbook.

The rabbit was a year and a half old when we turned him loose in the back yard. He had not seen another rabbit or any other animals since Joan adopted him. It was springtime and the sap was flowing. The rabbit fell in love with the hen.

At first the rabbit sniffed the hen and rubbed her with his nose, while the hen clucked nervously. But the rabbit was persistent. Finally he prevailed, mounting the hen. Soon she was laying eggs in a contented fashion. She even decided to set. We exchanged her eggs for some fertile ones.

The day came when three chicks hatched from the eggs we had given the hen. The rabbit remained attentive; the baby chickens perched on him even as he showered his attentions on their mother. When the mother strayed off, the rabbit would give shelter to the chicks. We saw, from the pair, how plastic were the biologic processes that constitute life, how adaptable young animals were, how totally amoral, in a sexual sense, were the ways of nature. It appeared, when one considered the homosexuality and intersexuality of animals, that conventional matings were but happy accidents that occurred in the course of sexual drives.

Imprintation is said to be different from the "associative" process by which we learn our lessons in school. There the more recently we have learned a lesson the better we remember it. But in imprintation it is not the most recent experience, it is the first that is best remembered. Also associative learning is reinforced by reward —the carrot in front of the donkey—while the reverse is true in imprintation. If a baby duckling has to struggle uphill over stones and sticks and gets pecked and beaten as it tries to follow its mother, the imprintation on her is not diminished but strengthened.

In spite of these purported differences there may be a time when the principles of imprintation and associative learning blend. Most of us have memories of early childhood that are more vivid than of things that happened yesterday. And people may be like the baby ducks that had to work so hard to follow their mother; they may learn better if the path is not too smooth and the reward not too immediate.

Psychologists are now studying the principles of imprintation under controlled conditions to try to see how long in life the phenomenon persists and whether there are periods in later life or in special fields of learning to which the principles of imprintation apply. Perhaps the facility of a young child to learn a language and speak it without an accent is an example. Perhaps there are similar periods that are best adapted to other types of learning, such as mathematics. Even such a function as the ability to make close friends seems to be placed in time so that the period in which the firmest friendships are made is apt to coincide roughly with the period in which a mate is usually chosen. In the wider application of the term, there remains much to be studied and learned about imprintation. Perhaps it was this principle that prompted the statement in Proverbs, "Train up a child in the way he should go: and when he is old he will not depart from it."

Imprintation is a biological principle that applies elsewhere than in a behavior of *individual* birds and animals. On one end of the spectrum it applies to the behavior of cells within an individual, and on the other to the behavior of social groups made up of many individuals.

The blood cells known as lymphocytes attack and destroy any cells that are foreign to the body. But these cells can be taught to accept and live in harmony with foreign cells that they normally attack. This is done by injecting cells from an animal of the same species into a newborn animal. After this, grafts from the animal whose cells were injected will survive. Induced tolerance this is called but, as in the case of imprintation, the foreign element must be introduced during a critical period of immaturity if tolerance is to be imprinted on the cell.

The same principle holds true in inducing tolerance into societies of animals and man. If a human society is young and immature, like a frontier society, or if it is a colony of animals that has been newly displaced from an old home, the organization of the society has not grown rigid and it may still be plastic in its acceptance of things that are new. Later, when the society is mature, its period of imprintation is past, and new ideas or foreign individuals are apt to be rejected.

Both the immune systems and the societies of man and animals must maintain a delicate balance. If they are too tolerant of things foreign, the body or the society may be attacked and destroyed by invasion from without. If they are too intolerant, they react so sharply against minor deviations that they may destroy their own body or their society by civil war.

"It would seem," Plato said, "that the directions in which education starts a man will determine his future life." If the principles of imprintation were applied sternly to the education of young children, there is little question that the direction of their lives and the development of the world could be changed. There are many such examples in history, from Sparta, through the Nazi movement, and lately in the communes of China. None of them to date have survived for long. Perhaps the molding of all to a single opinion results in fatal intolerance of evolution and change. The natural selection of ideas and the slow process of adaptation may be safer than a centralized educational system in which all are imprinted with identical doctrines.

In biological processes, including education, the time at which a stimulus is applied is apt to be as important as the nature of the stimulus. Imprintation is effective only during a brief period of an animal's life; chemical stimulation of various phases of growth and development must be timed with equal precision. If, at a certain time in the development of the embryo of a salamander, its tail is injected with a bit of dried brain tissue, the lens of an eye will develop at the site of the injection. The mysterious "inducer substances," each at a precise moment in the development of an embryo, act upon cells to determine how each type of cell will change and develop into its next phase. These "inducer substances" are effective only if they reach the cell at the exact time that it is ready for the transformation. The cell is like Cinderella's pumpkin; at the stroke of a wand it can be changed into a golden coach, but the stroke must be at precisely the right time, or nothing happens.

From the moment the egg cell is fertilized there ensues a series of transformations in the daughter cells that culminate in the production of a new individual. From the moment of its birth the new individual is subjected to a series of experiences that mold its patterns of behavior. From the moment the mature individual enters the society of the world, he molds and is molded by that society. If, at each phase of development from egg to emperor, the appropriate stimulus is received at the proper moment effective transformations can be wrought. This, at least, is what Gozzle and our animals seemed to be saying to Jane and me as we watched the interplay of their personalities in our yard.

2

CURRENTS
OF LIFE—
CANADA, 1936

See the rivers how they run
Changeless towards a changeless sea.

—Charles Kingsley

Throughout the years of our marriage Jane and I on vacations, and our children too, often traveled to out-of-the-way, distant places in search of the wilderness. There, and in later life we came face to face with nature's inexorable reality.

When difficult problems were forced upon us we believed that because we had been brought up and had spent so much time in natural surroundings, we adapted ourselves to unpleasant events more easily than we would have if, as children, we had experienced chiefly the rigid conformity of organized work and play. In nafor supper he brought out brown bread and a bucketful of big-egged, gray-black caviar, cool and delicious. We gave Ivan an Imperial quart of Canadian whiskey and he invited us to wash down the caviar with part of it. Ivan said he would tow our canoes down the lake with his powerboat the next morning.

The lake we were heading for was Lake Expanse, ten miles in diameter, deep, round, and famous for its sudden storms. There was no breath of wind and the surface was a mirror next morning as we putted down it in the powerboat. At noon, Ivan slowed down, threw the clutch out of gear, and pointed out an inlet three miles in the distance.

"That's the Winawash River where you want to go."

We pulled the canoes alongside and got into them. Ivan cruised away for his fishing grounds. We dipped our paddles in the smooth water, heading for the inlet.

Just five minutes after the powerboat had left us a dark cloud appeared. In five minutes more the northern sky was black. We were still a mile from shore when the wind hit. There was no use paddling against it. Jane and I tried but we saw that not even Tom and Peg could hold their own. Turning the canoes around and with the waves and wind behind us, we scooted across the lake, bailing and steering as best we could to keep out of the dangerous troughs of the waves.

The wind swept both canoes into a part of the lake that years before had been flooded by a hydroelectric dam and was now filled with dead fallen trees. The bow of our canoe ran up on the stump of one. Jane grabbed for its roots in the freezing water and held on while the boat swung around in the wind. Then down the wind we went again, tail first, until we hit another and it was my turn to grab and hang on. At length, half swamped, still bailing, we found ourselves being blown into a pocket of muskeg—a kind of bog, where blueberry bushes started from the water and rotten logs and debris floated in the scum of the sluggishly rolling waves. We were grateful for the haven but it had started to snow and there was no shore to be seen. We were completely lost.

It was getting colder all the time and night was coming on. The wind was still blowing and the waves were so high we were afraid we would be swamped if we left the shelter of the muskeg. The scummy water was only shoulder-deep but so near to freezing that we could not have survived in it for more than half an hour. Yet we had to get ashore while it was still light enough to see.

We steered our way through the sunken logs and branches. It was almost dark when we were blown up on the boggy mainland where scrubby, water-soaked pines tried to grow. We pulled up the canoes, unloaded them, and turned them over our duffel bags while Tom went to get wood for the fire. He handled his axe like an extension of his hand. In a few strokes he peeled the bark from a green birch tree. He split a dead cedar log in four and slivered the heart of it. He lit the birch bark and putting the cedar slivers in it, cupped his hands

Then suddenly we were free and we found that we could cook as well as a cook, that the children willingly helped in the work, that the family was self-sufficient. It was comfortable to find that we could dress up or down for dinner as we pleased.

The two years in California changed our way of living, and the animals that we kept reminded us of the pleasure that we had had in childhood from the close association with animals. It was this experience that prompted us, at last, to make a miniature Bonita out of our back yard in Cleveland.

California also changed our way of recreation. We had spent the weekends there on the beaches or in the sea with swim fins and flippers.

Jane's and my interest in diving had grown out of an experience that I had had as an eight-year-old. On a houseboat cruise with my family, Captain Dunn, co-inventor of the Miller Dunn diving hood, had let me down in the apparatus on a Florida coral reef. I was deeply affected by the experience, and never forgot that slow, unreal, weightless world of muted colors and floating shapes. It haunted me so that on our honeymoon I took Jane to the Florida Keys. As we looked down through the clear bright water, we decided that some day we would try to take pictures beneath the sea.

In California, Jane and I learned how to use face plates and flippers in diving. We improvised a waterproof casing for a motion picture camera and after the war, on a shallow reef in the Bahamas, we exposed a few reels of color film showing coral and a majestic black angel-fish. These were the first underwater moving pictures that we had seen and among the first ever made for public viewing. Back in Cleveland we showed and reshowed that movie to our friends.

Thereafter we spent our vacations—most of them with our children—making underwater movies which Jane used in film lectures and on television, both here and on programs of the British Broadcasting Corporation.

Since we wanted to tell our story in every medium, we also wrote about life beneath the sea, spearfishing, underwater photography, the finding of ancient shipwrecks in the Caribbean, and of adventures in the Mediterranean in search of underwater relics of the Romans and Greeks. Aside from medicine, underwater exploration became my dominant interest and as a result I became interested in writing of things other than science. Soon this was to have a profound effect on my professional career and eventually on Jane's survival. No matter where one starts in the web of human interests all is interrelated. Sooner or later each interest touches another and in touching it may bring it light.

The children were now in school and Jane had time for work outside the home. Writing and lecturing gave her a profession of her own. She had vigor and stamina, and when she went about giving her film lectures she lugged along not only a 16 mm. projector but an eight-foot screen, two big amplifiers, the heavy reels of film, a suitcase full of gadgets, and a tape recorder for the music—nearly 200 pounds of equipment. These she set up and tested herself, not letting anyone touch them. When introduced, she would stride to the stage, shake some undersea relic in the face of the audience, give her introduction, then return to her seat, turn on the projector, check its focus, start the music on the recorder, and read the script. It was a prestidigitator's feat, but she managed to do it, all the while speaking in a strong contralto voice.

We made several film lectures of our underseas adventures in the Caribbean, but Jane's and my first European trip together was in 1950. At that time the children ranged from four to fourteen and, not yet old enough to travel with us, could be left with a housekeeper. We decided to make a travel and adventure film on the island of Corsica and in the Mediterranean Sea. There we met Costa, a retired bandit, who introduced us to the friendly ways of the Corsican country people.

It started one May evening in Ajaccio, the capital of Corsica and the birthplace of Napoleon. It was the hour of the promenade when everyone went walking in the street. Jane and I stopped in at a small café, the *Bar de la Gaieté,* where we sat on blue metal chairs at a sidewalk table and ordered *pastis,* the licorice-tasting national drink. In a moment the door of the café swung open, and out strode the proprietor, imposing in brown corduroy, a heavy gold chain strung across his vest. He brought us our *pastis* in tall glasses and water to mix with it. Then we invited him to have a drink with us, and he got one and sat down to talk.

"I am Jacques Costa," he said, in French. "They

call me *le Roi des Sangliers,* the King of the Wild Boars. Come, let me show you what they look like."

Costa led us into the café and up to the bar. Behind it was a mirror and tucked into the frame were a group of enlarged photographs.

"These are *les sangliers,*" Costa said, pointing to the vicious-tusked wild boars covered with long black hair.

"When do you go to hunt *les sangliers?*" we asked. "We'd like to make a movie of the hunt and of the old Corsica, the way it used to be."

"Meet me here tomorrow morning early for coffee," Costa said. "My friends and I are leaving at five o'clock to hunt the boar in the *maquis.*"

We accepted, and at five o'clock the next morning were parking our rented four-horsepower Renault at the *Bar de la Gaieté.* Costa was awaiting us in the pale morning light. He was wearing the same brown corduroy, a tweed cap pulled low on his forehead and a black shirt. He had a brown, weather-worn, decorated gourd on a strap over his shoulder and his leather cartridge belt was filled with twelve-gauge shells.

"Buck shot," he told us, and indicated the size of the pellets.

He took us into the bar and gave us each a bowl of strong black coffee and a thick piece of brown bread. He reinforced his own coffee with a generous slug of *Cap Corse* brandy and swallowed the mixture in gulps. Picking up a heavy pistol, he tucked it into his cartridge belt, and shouldered a beautifully embossed double-barreled Belgian shotgun. Then he went to a back room of the bar and returned with his hunting dogs. They were shaggy-haired griffons named Moustache, Tango, and Pantero, and they looked like crosses between spaniels and poodles. They barked, straining at their leashes, pulling Costa out of the bar onto the street. He pointed to them. *"Rien de meilleur pour le sanglier,"* he said. "Nothing better for hunting a wild boar."

A long black limousine, suggestive of the ones in American gangster movies and filled with five fierce-faced men, roared up, swerved around our tiny Renault and stopped abruptly at the curb. Costa and the dogs leaped into the back of the limousine, and before I had time to focus my camera on them, the boar hunters, at a clip of a hundred kilometers per hour, started up the deserted *Cours de Napoléon.* We followed in the little Renault, which, with throttle open and going downhill, could hardly make a hundred kilometers. With a feeling of despair we saw the hunters draw away. But on the dirt roads at breakneck speed, we found that we could just keep up with the distant cloud of dust.

Soon the smooth road ended and we climbed into the hills in first gear, threading our way through flocks of goats and long-legged Corsican sheep. The limousine ahead swung off the road onto a goat path that zig-zagged back and forth over jagged stones and cactus. After two miles of this we stopped in a grove of eucalyptus trees, shading the ruins of a military outpost once used, we were later told, to control bandits. A lean shepherd of undefinable age, wearing a droopy handlebar moustache, got up from the ruins. He pushed his floppy, black hat onto the back of his head and muttered the Corsican equivalent of, "Where the devil have you been?" With the shepherd was a heavy-set peasant who looked to be in his sixties, dressed in the pale blue working clothes we had seen on the Corsican farmers. Costa pointed at the peasant and said, "Pogliani—*Le Prince des Sangliers.*" Pogliani, like Costa, wore a tweed cap, and carried a gun; it was an ancient hammerlock that might have been a relic of the *Grande Armée* of Napoleon. His dog, Cobra, held by a rope, was of mixed ancestry, but Costa said he also was *rien de meilleur pour le sanglier.*

The hunters, who had piled out of the limousine, gathered in a circle and talked loudly. We understood little of the Corsican tongue, although it resembled French enough so that we caught occasional familiar words and got the gist of the conversation. Costa tied tiny bells to the collars of his three griffons. They barked and Cobra joined them. The men began shouting and gesticulating and pointing to all quarters of the compass. We gathered that there were signs of wild boar. Also someone had seen a rabbit and the hunters were afraid the dogs would chase the rabbit instead of the boar.

The hunters scrambled single file up a precipitous trail, old Pogliani leading the way like a mountain goat. Jane and I panted in the rear and paused from time to time to take pictures. The path twisted and turned. Soon we were enclosed, above and below, in the thorny, sweet-scented, flowering *maquis* that Napoleon, in exile, so well remembered in his dreams. Covering the hills, against the dark green background of ferns and fir-like *bruyère,* were white flowering hawthorn and cistus, purple thistles, golden mimosa, and a profusion of daisies, poppies, primroses, and cyclamen. Far below we could see the Gulf of Ajaccio, bright as a jewel, lapping at the feet of the hills.

We went at a steady, rapid pace. At each turn of the trail a surprise awaited us. A cow went dashing into the bushes, a lizard slithered across the trail, a tiny snake took shelter beneath a stone. We passed horses and colts running wild in the *maquis;* a partridge rose with drumming wings; inquisitive donkeys looked at us from a jungle of flowers. Through every break in the *maquis,* we caught glimpses of blue mountains with snow-capped peaks. All these things we were trying desperately to photograph and still keep up with the hunters.

The trail leveled off along a ridge. *Le sanglier,* Pogliani said, will *passe par là* and he pointed to a path which crossed ours. Costa told us to remain with Pogliani, and guard the pass-point in the trail; then he disappeared with the hunters in the *maquis.* We could hear them crashing through the thorny barrier that for a century sheltered the Corsican bandits. For a few moments we could hear the snapping of twigs as the men tramped on up the mountainside. Then all was silent, and we three were alone.

"What is *le sanglier* like?" Jane whispered. "How big is he?"

Pogliani whispered back, "Very big and black, and

he has a long nose. Waist high he stands, and weighs two hundred pounds."

"Will he attack us?"

"He kills men not very often, but sometimes he kills the dogs who track him through the *maquis*." Then the old hunter told us that the dogs are trained to grab the boar by the ear or by the testicles, and hold on so they keep clear of his tusks. Later when the boar is killed, the dogs bite the back of his neck and scalp him. "But now silence," Pogliani said, "we must listen for the boar. You will hear the 'tucka-tucka-tucka' of his feet."

We waited but heard only the buzz of bumblebees, the repetitive cry of invisible cuckoos, and the burring sound of the arundel birds. We were getting sleepy, lulled by the perfume and stillness. We were dozing in the shade when the first far-off bay of one of the hounds came.

The baying came closer. There was shouting from the mountain top. Pogliani was on his feet, cocking his ancient hammerlock with his thumb. Cobra whined and strained at the rope. The two stood ready at the intersection of the trail. Jane and I focused our cameras. There was a stirring in the underbrush and the "tucka-tuck-tucka" of small hard feet. The *maquis* waved; the bushes parted. Pogliani sighed and uncocked his gun. Out of the bushes came a pair of slender horns and a Satanic face, bearded and black, the eyes bright and impish. The little goat shook its head, and bounding across the trail, disappeared into the *maquis*. It was as though we had caught a glimpse of Pan.

Pogliani shrugged, glancing at the noonday sun.
"No good for boar any more," he said. "The ground is
too hot to hold the scent. It is time to eat." We were glad
to hear there would be food, and at once forgot our disappointment about the boar hunt.

We put our cameras on our shoulders again and
followed our guide, stopping from time to time to photograph Pogliani against the *maquis* and the distant blue
of the bay.

He led us down the mountain across a valley to a
square, stone house beside an enormous acacia tree. Its
shade, after the over-dry heat of the *maquis,* was as re-
freshing as a pool in a mountain stream.

At a long table beneath the tree, Costa and the
other hunters were already seated on benches. *Le patron,* Monsieur Minherra, was a stout, white-haired
shepherd who wore what seemed to be the traditional
Corsican hunting suit of brown corduroy. About his
middle was the scarlet sash of the *Grande Armée.* He
motioned us to seats, poured each of us an ounce or two
of *pastis* and filled the glasses with water. The clear
yellow liquid turned white and opaque. The drink was
smooth; the shade was cool.

After the fourth or fifth *pastis,* the men began to
talk more freely. They discussed bandits. Costa took off
his gourd, which he had been carrying as a canteen, and
laid it on the table. Burned into its side was the face of a
ferocious bearded man. Costa pointed to it. *"C'est le
bandit Paoletti.* This is a bandit who lived here in these
hills. Once this was Paoletti's gourd. I was often of

service to him, and after he was killed it was his son who gave me this gourd."

"Times have changed," said *le patron* sadly. "Once, if a man was not a bandit, he was not a man *de bon coeur*. No longer is there *la licence du maquis*."

"Yes," said Pogliani, "freedom as well as honor is gone from the hills."

The men talked on of the days in which Corsica was dominated by leaders defiant of the laws of France. They told of the bandit Romanetti, a Corsican Robin Hood, loved by the peasants and feared by the law. During the most glorious days of banditry, Costa said, more than fifteen hundred *gendarmes* combed the *maquis* for some two hundred bandits. Then when Romanetti's daughter was married a truce was declared and a great feast given to which all the important people of Corsica came. The *gendarmes*, too, were there. Of course, on the following day, the chase of Romanetti was resumed.

"Did they catch him?" Jane asked.

"No," Pogliani replied, and explained that the peasants were the bandits' friends and saw to it that they were seldom caught behind the barriers of the *maquis*. It was not until the bandits grew overbearing and began to interfere in the politics of the people that many of them, like Romanetti, were slain, not by the police, but by the peasants who once had been their friends.

The *pastis* bottle made the rounds again. From a shed beside the house, where an old woman in black was stirring an ancient pot, came clouds of steam and the

smell of cooking meat. A dark Corsican girl with large
eyes brought a platter of hors d'oeuvres: sliced tomatoes, radishes, and tiny wrinkled olives. With her was
her son, a flaxen-haired, blue-eyed boy of eight whom
they called Charley. It was just nine years since the
American occupation of Corsica, and we thought of the
countless waves of seaborne invasions which, from the
beginnings of medieval history, had broken over Corsica's coasts. From the days of the Phoenicians, Corsica
had been occupied in turn by Ligurians, Greeks, Etrus-
cans, Carthaginians, Romans, Vandals, Byzantines,
Saracens, Moors, Genoese, Pisans, English, Germans,
Italians, French, and Americans, and had been subject,
besides, to the raids of Mediterranean pirates. Though
the coastlines had been captured, the inhabitants of the
interior never had been subjugated. They retained the
fierce independence of the peoples of the hills.

"We like you Americans," *le patron* said, and he
opened a bottle of *vin rosé*. The bright wine gurgled
into the glasses and we proposed a toast to Corsica.

"*À la Corse*," the hunters cried, and as we caught
the light bouquet of the wine, we stood and raised our
glasses.

"*À la Corse*," we shouted back, "*au sanglier*." We
had become a part of this bright, warm land.

Le patron's daughter, Suzette, flashing-eyed and
olive-skinned, brought *prosciutto*—thin slices of wild
boar ham, dark red, lean, and flavored, like all Corsican
ham, by the herbs of the *maquis* on which the boars had
foraged. The ham was neither cooked nor smoked;

it was raw, salted heavily, and had hung for six months in a cave. As we washed down the ham with carafes of Corsican wine, the conversation turned to children. We said we had four. Costa announced that he had twelve children and kept them all under the table, pointing to his dogs.

"Treize," said one of his friends. "You forget the one on your belly."

"Yes, that is right, I have thirteen children," said Costa. One is on my belly."

"Show them. Show them," cried Pogliani.

With a retired bandit's equivalent of a blush, Costa stripped to the waist. Across his ample belly ranged the blue tattoo of a griffon hunting dog. Moustache looked up from under the table and whined, jealous, at his image.

"This mark," Costa said, pointing to a blue, indelible, unwinking eye on his arm, "was made in Singapore." Beneath it, in blurred script, was written *"victime des yeux de la police."* "I am a victim of the police's eyes," Costra translated.

"What were you doing in Singapore?" Jane asked.

Costa refilled his wine glass. "In Singapore I had a little bar-café." He looked back nostalgically through the decades. "Ah, that was a life, in Singapore, but then there was the trouble."

Before he could tell us about the trouble, *le patron* pointed to Costa's left buttock. *"Montrez, montrez,"* he urged. "Show them what is there. It came from Singapore, too."

"That I cannot show you," Costa said. "But I will tell you that it is a pretty picture of a gendarme hanging by the neck."

Across Costa's hairy chest he exhibited his tattooed motto: *"Je n'ai peur de rien."* "I fear nothing." It was made in Jibouti, he told us.

"It was in Jibouti that a comrade of mine introduced me to your great American bandit, Al Capone," he said, respect in his voice. "I did a favor for your American bandit and he gave me a little machine gun that would shoot fifty rounds. You know Monsieur Capone?"

No, we never met him, we said. Costa looked sad.

The tattoos with which Costa was covered came also from Saigon, Algiers and Port Said. A few were from Marseilles. At the word Marseilles, everyone at the table reached for his glass.

"Au vieux port," said Pogliani. "Let's drink to the old port." The dark-skinned Suzette, who seemed well acquainted with the Marseilles waterfront, filled a glass and joined the men in a toast to Corsica's favorite city.

"Ah, the life in Marseilles! Those were in the days before I married," said Pogliani.

"If you had the price of a cup of chocolate," Costa said, "that was *assez pour la femme*. If you had the price of a roast goat—ah! then you could have a harem."

"It was at Marseilles that I met my wife," said *le patron* moodily, "and then it was the end—*tout fini*."

Suzette joined in the conversation, but by Corsican tradition she stood beside the table and did not sit with the men. The men told of the wonders of the old port. Like veterans reminiscing of a famous campaign, they boasted of their affairs with women and with the police.

Suzette interrupted by serving a *pâté de merle.* It was old King Cole's favorite dish made of ground-up blackbirds; they had been snared in horsehair loops that were set in the arbutus trees of the *maquis.* It tasted like a delicate *paté de foie gras* but lighter, like the blackbirds' song. The wine flasks were refilled. Then conversation ceased and all concentrated on an enormous golden-yellow omelet with white curds in its center and generously flavored with wild mint from the *maquis.* The smell of roasting meat became stronger, and the old woman put a forked stick under the handle of the black pot, carried it out, and set it steaming on the table. It was a quarter of a goat, a *cabri,* forty days old, roasted with young potatoes and basted for hours with white wine and wild herbs. It was golden brown, tender as a chicken, and sweet. With it, on the same plate with the meat, came a fresh, green salad dressed with olive oil, vinegar, and *romarin,* the sage of the *maquis.*

When it seemed that *le patron's* resources must be exhausted, there appeared the *spécialité de la maison:* a bowl full of *broussie,* made from the curdled milk of the *brebis,* those tall, thin, sad-faced sheep that are raised mainly for their rich milk. Each of them gives about a pint a day. Milking the *brebis* is an art; each drop is squeezed from the tiny teats between the tip of the thumb and the index finger. Most of the milk is made into Corsican cheese which is exported to France, ripened in caves, and sold as Roquefort. The rest is eaten fresh in the form of this *broussie*.

Each of us had a plateful of *broussie* covered with sugar and doused with *Rhum St. James* from Martinique. We washed it down with black coffee, the beans freshly ground, and with Corsican *eau de vie* distilled in a copper cauldron from *le patron's* own grapes. When the *eau de vie* glasses were empty, they were refilled, first with white grapes soaked in *eau de vie,* and then with prunes doused in cognac.

The hunt breakfast had lasted all afternoon. We pushed back the bench and fed the dogs the scraps. The sunlight was slanting low beneath the dark green leaves of the huge acacia tree. From the heart of the *maquis* came the braying of a donkey and the cuckoo's evening song. There were further pledges of eternal friendship, solemn goodbyes. We promised to return again to hunt *le sanglier.*

"Did you get the cinema you wanted?" Costa asked us.

I put my arm around him and glowingly assured him that we did.

"Vous êtes bien tombés," Costa told us. "You fell in the right place. If you were looking for the old Corsica, you found it."

We followed the hunters' long black limousine down from the *maquis* at an uneven, rapid pace until it disappeared in the distance and dust. We sang and laughed and agreed that this had been the finest hunt breakfast we ever heard of. Groves of olive trees gleamed on the hillside by the winding road. At last we reached a beach of golden sand beside the blue expanse of the Bay of Ajaccio.

I slammed on the brakes. The Renault swerved off the road to a standstill. "Look at that poppy, Jane!"

I leaped out, camera in hand, and approached the flower on hands and knees. "This will be the most beautiful picture we've ever brought back," I declared.

Later, back in Cleveland, we put the film on the projector and a blur of unfocused scarlet filled our screen. We laughed, for we remembered that poppy in the sweet-smelling *maquis,* and it reminded us of the *eau de vie* and the hospitality of Costa and his friends to a pair of strangers from a distant foreign land.

4

VIVE
LE TARN—
FRANCE, 1954

*The soul of a journey is liberty,
perfect liberty to think, feel,
and do just as one pleases.*

—William Hazlitt

The behavior patterns of many animals are so
built into them by heredity that they are rigid and unchangeable. A swallow's nest always looks like a swallow's nest no matter how the bird was brought up. But
man inherits few patterns of behavior; most of them are
acquired. His mind, in contrast to that of most animals,
is able to adapt. Nevertheless, the patterns of behavior
that are learned in youth, the preferences, the prejudices,
and the habits of dependency or of self-reliance, are apt
to remain fixed for a lifetime.

Everyone who has raised either animals or children
is aware that different individuals exposed to the same

influences do not necessarily react in the same way. Even identical twins, raised in the same family, may develop striking differences in personality. Two rabbits born in the same litter and raised together show individualistic patterns of behavior. Out of a dozen laboratory mice inbred to be so identical that they accept transplants of one another's tissues, one or two may react in a different way from the others in the experiment. There are differences in the chemistries of bodies and minds that are too subtle to be detected except as they influence behavior.

For imprintation to be most effective in an animal, it is necessary not only to provide a substitute for the natural mother, but also, as the natives of South America did with their sheep dogs, to isolate the baby from its litter-mates or peers. Otherwise there creeps into the patterns of behavior, the effect of the interplay of personalities, the variations that are produced by two individuals, as in ping-pong, batting back and forth observations and ideas. That is why education is different from imprintation. The wide range of experiences and concepts that are met in education bring out individualities instead of suppressing them as may be done when the principle of imprintation is effectively used.

Jane and I had no fear of impressing our children too heavily with the love of an outdoor life. Vacations were too short for that, and there were too many other influences at work. What we wanted to do was to use the vacation time to show them a different way of life. We wanted them to be imprinted early with the self-reliance that comes from living in the out-of-doors. For a time, the younger ones were too small to travel well. Later, we knew the older ones would become involved in their own affairs. In between, there was a period when our family could travel together as a unit. We took them on canoe trips in Canada, pack trips in the West, and diving expeditions in the Caribbean. When the three older ones were studying French we went to southern France to kayak down the gorges of the Tarn. It was the first trip abroad for the children. It was also the last that all of us were able to take together.

We first heard about the Tarn River at dinner with Philippe Diole, the French underwater explorer, archeologist, and author, who had paddled the full twenty-six hundred miles of the Niger River in western Africa, alone. We told him our family was planning a canoe trip in France.

He leaned across the table, energy bursting from his massive shoulders and round, radiant face. *"Bon.* It is to the Grand Canyon of southern France you must go. You must shoot the gorges of the Tarn."

Jane asked him to tell about the gorges.

"The Tarn is *fourmillant de rapides*—boiling with rapids," Diole said, and added that we ought not try the rapids in rigid canoes but in light, collapsible kayaks that we could carry with us in our car.

We had never thought of a kayak except as a seal-skin boat into which Eskimos laced themselves when they wanted to go walrus hunting in the Bering Sea. "We'll do it," I said for both of us.

It was four months later, in June, that we started off to explore the Tarn, in our train the four children—Ann now nineteen, Joan sixteen, Susie eleven, and nine-year-old George—and also Peggy French, a classmate of Joan's. It was a carefree, noisy group dressed in camp clothes, with spare things packed in small red duffel bags, one apiece. Jane and I had a waterproof bag for our camera equipment, for we were making a movie of the trip. In Lyons we rented a car and bought three collapsible kayaks. We put them together in the square of the red-roofed village of Sainte Enimie.

A crowd, made up largely of old men and young boys, gathered to watch the struggle and advise us as we sweated and strained at the struts and the rubber-coated canvas. It had taken the salesman at Martin Sports Shop in Lyons twenty minutes to put one of the kayaks together, disassemble it, and pack it with the others on top of the Chevrolet. But it took us over three hours to fit all the overgrown bones into the stiff new skins of our kayaks. We stripped the threads on four bolts. Susie fell into her kayak and broke one of the ribs.

It was high noon by the time we had the kayaks assembled and our baggage locked in the car. A road followed the river and there were buses on it, so that when we stopped for the night one of us could go back to get the car. The hot June sun was dazzling as we carried our kayaks across the white pebbled beach and slipped them into the green water of the Tarn. The kayaks were fifteen feet long, with brilliant orange decks, pale cloud-blue cockpits, and tiny red-white-and-blue French flags fluttering over their bows.

We waded into the water, climbed in and sat with legs outstretched feeling the motion of the water through the thin canvas skins. The kayaks, light and responsive, fitted us as though we were wearing them. We shoved off with our double-bladed paddles, the current took us, and we were a part of the moving stream. Jane and I were in one kayak; Ann, Susie, and George in another; and in the last, Joan and Peggy. Blue sky was above, beneath an emerald river, ahead of us the unknown.

The river, twenty yards across, flowed swiftly, sparkling and gurgling over the pebbly bottom. The water was clear as a spring's. Schools of trout fanned out and scattered like bomb bursts at our bows.

"It's like riding in a Thunderbird," Joan shouted as she and Peggy shot by us in the easy side-to-side swing of their double-bladed paddles.

George, only his face and blond crew-cut showing, was tucked in between Susie and Ann in the lead boat. Their kayak was as accommodating as Bayard, the mythical horse who could stretch his body to carry any number of children. But the three of them could not synchronize their paddles, and kept blocking one another's strokes. They laughed and hooted as the boat skittered down the river like an untrained colt.

The Canoe Club of France had given us a river guide and a *carte nautique* which mapped the rapids and classified the rivers according to their difficulties from class I—safe for beginners, to class IV and V—for experts only. The Tarn was classified partly II and mostly III. Diagrams explained how best to shoot the rapids, but it was not in a charted rapid that the first accident occurred. Just above the bridge and out of control, Ann's kayak whammed into the only boulder in sight. As the boat swung broadside, Susie caught her paddle on the rock. The blade snapped in two, the boat tipped and teetered; it spun around and went stern first downstream. A gay crowd cheered from the bridge and laughed at Susie, squealing and paddling with the broken half of her paddle.

Through the medieval arch of the bridge, the valley opened ahead of us. There were steep, terraced vineyards, jutting crags of windworn rock, and gray stone houses growing from the water's edge. The current swept us along so all we had to do was steer. High above were the ruins of an abbey. Ahead, in a bend of the river, was the "amphitheater of healing" known as the *Cirque des Baumes,* to which, in the Middle Ages, the sick journeyed from all over France to be healed through the power of Sainte Enimie.

Down the river the steady current swept us, past farms and villages, over shoals and through swirling pools until we came to a place where the stream swung fast and foaming close to a high bank from which a tree had fallen partly into the water.

"Pull to the right!" Jane warned the children behind us, as we cleared the tree and rounded the bend.

roy pants and coarse blue shirts stood on the seats and were poling up the stream with wooden staffs tipped with brass.

"You are Dutch?" one asked us.

"No, American," we called.

"Ah, *les Américains,* they too are the great *voyageurs,*" and his weatherbeaten face broke into a smile.

"Where are you taking the cherries?" we asked.

"To Sainte Enimie," the bowman said. "But there is no good market on the Tarn. Life is *très pénible,* very hard. We must live from the few fruits and grapes we raise in our shallow soil."

The man in the stern motioned to our kayaks to draw closer alongside, and they gave us all handfuls of cherries, sweet and warm from the sun. We offered payment but they refused. We thanked them and fell again into the rhythm of our paddling.

We were willing to go on for hours when George suddenly mentioned supper. Immediately all were ravenous and began to look along the banks for a place to eat and spend the night. Then Susie pointed ahead. High on the bank was a castle, with turrets, a moat and a drawbridge, its ramparts rising sheer from the water of the Tarn. We beached our kayaks just above the castle, and in the slanting rays of the evening sun, scrambled up the bank.

We had learned from the *carte nautique* that the castle, known as the *Château de la Case,* had been converted to an inn. The proprietor, Monsieur Jean Lepinc, met us with gestures of welcome, his black beret cocked over his ear. He escorted us across the lichen-covered drawbridge and through dark cobblestoned hallways to our rooms. Jane's and mine was a turret-curved chamber with mullioned windows and an enormous four-poster bed canopied in scarlet brocade. The children too were put up in great chambers all made of stone.

Monsieur Lepinc told us that seven centuries ago there had lived there eight beautiful maidens known as the "Nymphs of the Tarn." Their father had built and fortified this chateau to protect his daughters from the advances of lovers. Monsieur Lepinc then showed us the portraits of the "Nymphs" painted in 1641 on the ceiling of an octagonal chamber. The prim, stern-faced women wore long, puffed-sleeved, high-collared dresses and enormous black hats and scowled down on us severely.

"They look cross," said George.

"Nevertheless four were borne off by lovers," the proprietor assured us.

"Perhaps they had qualities that do not show in the picture," Jane said.

Above the castle was the road, blasted and tunneled through the rock. The proprietor told Joan and Peggy where to catch the bus back to the car in Sainte Enimie. They left and returned with our baggage in time for dinner.

Dinner was served by candle-light, in what was once a stone-arched chapel. There were *escargots,* their shells overflowing with parsley and garlic butter; there was *coq au vin,* and since it was mid-June we were given *fraises du bois,* the small, pungent wild strawberries of France.

After dinner, Jane and I had a glass of cognac with Monsieur Lepinc and he taught us a drinking song. The whole family roared it out:

> *Chevaliers de la table ronde,*
> *Goûtons voir si le vin est bon,*
> *Goûtons voir, oui, oui, oui,*
> *Goûtons voir, non, non, non!*
>
> *Knights of the round table,*
> *Let's taste and see if the wine is good,*
> *Let's taste and see, yes, yes, yes,*
> *Let's taste and see, no, no, no!*

The proprietor also told us of the Beast of the Guevaudan who was wont to prowl, the legendary wolf of the Cevennes who "ate women and children and shepherdesses celebrated for their beauty." As he talked the wind was moaning around the castle walls.

"Are there ghosts too?" Susie asked hopefully.

"Shhh," Monsieur Lepinc answered. "We don't speak of them. There are some who do not understand."

When Jane and I climbed into our four-poster that night, it sounded as if all the Beasts of the Cevennes were hunting their prey. A gigantic bat flew out of the canopy and we went after it with shouts and yells. The children heard us and came rushing from their rooms. We threw bolsters at it, heaved shoes, and tried to net it with sheets from the bed. Silently, it darted, at last, through the doorway and into the cobblestoned corridor's gloom. We retired to our separate beds.

The next morning the sun was bright and the river went swirling and sparkling past the castle. It felt good to get back into the kayak. By now each of the boats had developed its own personality; one had a patch, one a broken strut, the third had lost its tiny flag. As we started down the river we sang, shouting to the rhythm of our paddles:

> *Goûtons voir, oui, oui, oui,*
> *Goûtons voir, non, non, non!*

We passed, a mile on our way, a stone house built on the river's edge. A man and a woman waved to us from the balcony, and gesturing with bottle and glass offered us a drink. We stopped singing and shouted to them as, in the grip of the current, we were swept, dry-mouthed and disappointed, down the next rapid.

A few miles further, at the village of La Malene, we let our kayaks down over an old mill dam. Then we beached them in the shadow of a crested castle. At an orange and white parasoled table, we ate six-inch trout fresh from the Tarn, four apiece, crisply fried and served with a Mornay sauce. We hurried back to the canoes, for the *carte nautique* showed that we were about to start down the gorges, a difficult passage that we had to get through before dark.

The stream swept into the narrows where vertical cliffs of honey-colored chalk rose sixteen hundred feet from the water's edge. Subterranean streams burst from the cliffs and cascaded white and foaming into the green water of the Tarn. In places the water lay deep and still. We glided by dark, mysterious caverns, where shadows darted on the floor of moss and rocks and ferns. We knew that here the bones of prehistoric men had been found. Perhaps they were the same men who painted on the walls of the famous Lascaux caves nearby. The current caught us again, and we were whirled past great chunks of the cliff that had fallen into the stream.

Gradually the banks grew less sheer. Weird dolomitic formations eroded by water and wind made grotesque figures beneath which we paddled until, above the rapids of *Pas de Souci,* we had to pull our kayaks out of the river. There with raw violence the Tarn flowed under a rock slide with a hoarse roar. Legend said that here Sainte Enimie chased Satan screaming into the bowels of the earth, thus causing the chaotic slide that blocked the stream. It was the only portage that we had to make on our journey on the Tarn.

We carried the kayaks up to the road and walked to the nearby village where we were able to hire a truck to carry the kayaks three miles down the road to where the water became navigable again. We launched them beneath a Romanesque bridge and down the widening river we paddled into the broad valley below. The *carte nautique* had told us that some of the rapids ahead were class III, dangerous, and should be reconnoitered. This would be *le jour le plus sportif.*

The names of the rapids on the Tarn were provocative: *Les Pas de Loup*—the pass of the wolf, *Le Petit*

Pas de Souci—the little pass of worry, *Les Rapides de la Chanterelle*—with imagery of singing water. In the beginning of the trip, because the children had never shot such rough rapids, Jane and I had gone ahead and shouted directions, "Pull right, pull left! Look out for the rock!" All but Susie caught on pretty well. She continued lightheartedly to mix up left and right and half of the time pulled the wrong way.

By now the children knew that at the start of a rapid there was a chance to control their kayaks but once they were in its grip it had a mind of its own. The water took them where it wanted. All they could do was help their boats follow the deep channel of the stream, the black V that went down the middle of the white water. Then, if they were lucky, they were in the crested waves, riding them like a bronco.

At the top of the *Pas de la Fon* rapid, where the water spouted black into the white-waved chute, stood a huge, round boulder. Jane and I landed on it to reconnoiter the formidable rapid ahead. We saw that the mainstream of the chute was broken by a series of jagged rocks that swung the current far to the left under an overhanging bank. We got back into our kayak, shoved off, followed the left-hand side of the stream, and pulled up below the rapid on a sandbar.

We shouted over the roar of the rapid to the children to follow the same course that we had, far to the left. Twenty yards above the rapids, Joan's and Peggy's kayak began to pick up speed. The dark current caught it, and soon the kayak was going faster than the current. They shot by the boulder, paddles in the air, letting the water take control. Then the orange deck of the kayak disappeared under white water. It came up, headed straight for the jagged rocks. Peggy, in the bow, pulled left, Joan pried right, and the kayak sideslipped around the rocks, banked the turn where the water ran under the cliff, broke out of the main current and pulled up in the slowly whirling scud of the eddy below.

Now Ann, with George and Susie, was at the barrier. As they gathered speed their kayak headed straight for one of the rocks. "Pull left," Ann screamed. Susie pulled right. The kayak made a neat landing, broadside on the rock.

"Jump out on the rock and pull us around," Ann shouted to George, and she balanced the boat to keep its upstream gunnel high. George scrambled out on the slippery boulder, and at once Ann and Susie were whirled into the current, back end to. With roller-coaster screams, they shot backwards into the white water of the chute and under the overhanging bank. The kayak bounced off, bumped along the shallows, and miraculously still afloat, ended up half full of water in the eddy.

We tossed George, left on the rock in the middle of the stream, our letdown rope and pulled him across the current to the shore. When we reached the bottom of the rapids, we were all as soaked as though we had been in the water with George.

We continued on our way wet and, as the day advanced, hungry. We had had no lunch, and were on the lookout for a place to eat. At midafternoon we passed lines of bed sheets drying on the bank. We thought there must be an inn and parked our kayaks. We followed a trail up the wooded bank and there we came upon the Grand Hôtel du Rozier.

On a balcony surrounded by climbing roses in full bloom, we were served by a good-natured chef with a white hat and a waxed moustache. We ate continually for almost two hours. The hors d'oeuvres were tiny black olives, *pâté de foie gras,* red and shiny thin-sliced sausage, broiled tomatoes with cheese sauce, and hard-boiled eggs covered with the chef's own mayonnaise. Then a large omelet with a white cheese sauce of mushrooms and *crevettes*—tiny shrimp. To the delight of the children, who had eaten them in Canada, the chef next brought in *grenouilles sautées,* frogs' legs fried in butter with parsley and a squeeze of lemon.

Clean plates were brought; on them was white asparagus—long, cold, fat, sweet and soft. With this was a dry white wine with which we drank toasts. Next, welcomed by cries from the children, we were given filet mignon, charcoal-broiled, juicy and rare, with puffy French fried potatoes on the side. With this we had a local red wine, sparkling in the sunlight, with a Burgundy bouquet. Dessert was a basket of ripe yellow plums and big cherries, and cheese from the nearby caves of Roquefort. Our coffee was made in individual drip pots perched on each person's cup. The patron and the chef seemed to enjoy our pleasure as much as we.

We spent that night in a room high over the river

bank and fell asleep to the soft music of the stream. It was a sad sound for it reminded us that the next day was to be our last on the Tarn. The river had been good to us. It had made the children, in their own canoes, reliant on themselves, it had introduced us to friendly strangers and to the pleasant customs of a foreign land. Regretfully in the morning we started down the widening, calming stream, where for long stretches there was little current. Soon the signs of the city of Millau began to appear—electric cables crossed the stream, there were houses on the bank, and people passed us in rowboats and canoes. The *carte nautique* advised disembarking at a dam a mile above the city but it did not say why. In the mid-afternoon we came to the dam, and looked over it onto a calm navigable stream that ran into the heart of the city. We decided that, rather than carry the kayaks and walk to town, we'd take them around the dam and paddle on down the stream.

We knew that Millau was an industrial city filled with tanneries and glove factories. Two hundred yards below the dam the green water suddenly changed to a soupy brown. From the right bank a stream of red water two yards wide fell like a river of blood into the Tarn. Guts of animals floated by. The sparkling emerald river became a sluggish cesspool, stinking with tannery waste. We paddled through the refuse of this Stygian stream and at last landed beneath a twenty-foot stone bank in the center of the town. We hoisted the kayaks up into a shady park, borrowed a hose, and scrubbed the rock-scarred canvases clean, tucked them away in their green canvas sacks, and packed them into the car that Ann had already brought back from the last stop.

We had become so attached to our kayaks that instead of selling them back to the sports shop we shipped them home to Cleveland. One of the them we put on the rafters of a sun room that overlooks our garden and the pond, and it is still there.

Sometimes in the spring floods or after big summer rains the children have taken the kayaks and run the rapids of our local streams. There they discovered that the people they met along the Ohio rivers were just as friendly and hospitable as the people along the Tarn. Perhaps that was because the children, after their experiences in France, were looking for friendliness.

It had often seemed to Jane and me that we were able to find in people much of what we set out to find. Sometimes it took a little time to gain the confidence of strangers, for each people had customs that had been deeply imprinted upon them in childhood. We had noticed the same behavior among the waterfowl of our back yard. It always took a few days before a new duck found its place in the flock. When he did, it was as we had found it in the gorges of the Tarn. Acceptance was apt to be complete.

THE SPICE
OF DANGER—
SILVER SHOALS, 1955

I love to sail forbidden seas
and land on barbarous coasts.

—Herman Melville,
Moby Dick

One afternoon in our back yard a small banty
hen that we kept to hatch and raise baby wood ducks
helped a duck drive off a huge Pekin drake that was
molesting the duck's newly hatched brood. The banty bit
the drake and jumped on him with her little claws. She
had developed a maternal instinct for ducklings that
spilled over into the fearless defense of any duck's
brood. If the banty had not raised ducklings, she would
never have bothered to attack the drake.

Courage, whether it be in people or in hens, de-
pends a lot on background, training, and motivation. A

friend of ours was staying at Volcano Inn overlooking the crater of "The Big Island," Hawaii, when unexpectedly the volcano erupted. Our friend fled to the airport to charter a plane. It was useless to try to leave. The planes had all taken off for Honolulu to pick up Hawaiians who were bidding against one another to get planes to take them *to* the volcano. To each person his own dangers, his own delights.

Jane was more used to danger than I. Before we married she had learned to fly and had had her share of trouble including a dead-stick landing on her second solo flight. It isn't that people ever get used to being afraid. It's that after a lot of frightening experiences they no longer panic, and they become expert at concealing their feelings. Jane and I had got so good at this that we fooled even each other when we went diving for treasure on Silver Shoals. And later it would stand us in good stead when the threat to life became more precise.

When Jane and I set out for Silver Shoals we met Ed and Marion Link at Cap Haitien, Haiti. We were going in their boat, the *Sea Diver*. Ed, the inventor of the Link trainer for airplane pilots, was tall and hawk-faced, with a stern bearing that made you know who the captain was. Marion was a writer. In 1948 when we had first met them, they were yachters and had joined us in Florida to salvage the wreck of the eighteenth-century British man-of-war, H.M.S. *Looe*. They became expert divers and were knowledgeable in archeology as well.

We joined them in many expeditions in search of sunken treasure in the Bahamas and the Florida Keys.

When the Links had got interested in diving they outfitted a sixty-five-foot diesel-powered trawler with everything divers might need for salvage. The *Sea Diver* was equipped with radar, sonar, loran direction finder, air compressors, airlifts, jet pumps, heavy winches. In the engine room Ed Link had a shop in which he could build new parts to replace any that broke. He ran the ship and Marion did the cooking. The crew were two: a Bahamian fisherman named Kemp, who could read the bottom through fifty feet of water but could not run a motor; and Vidal, the Link's Canadian guide, who had never before been to sea.

At Cap Haitien where we met the *Sea Diver*, Jane and I spent just enough time to climb to the top of King Christophe's mile-high citadel, one of the world's most magnificent ruins. From its summit we looked across the mountain peaks to the blue stretches of the Caribbean. Over the horizon lay our goal—the treasure-laden Silver Shoals.

We boarded the *Sea Diver*, and as we left port we watched the peaks of Haiti's mountains vanish in the evening haze. We felt that we were sailing away from security. We knew that no one aboard but Ed could navigate or run the machinery or get us home. Ahead in the gathering dusk lay the oily reaches of the Sargasso Sea. In the vast clots of weed that floated in the slowly whirling vortex between the great oceanic currents of

north and south, all the eels of the Atlantic came to
breed. Here, legend said, the *Flying Dutchman* still
sailed. Here too, the weather of the west Atlantic was
made and most of its hurricanes born.

Link, in the pilot house, had taken out a modern
chart and was checking it against the chart in William
Phipps' diary. The diary was written in 1686 when
Phipps salvaged the wreck of the *Golden Lion,* a Span-
ish galleon laden with three hundred tons of silver and a
fortune in gold and jewels. On her, legend says, was a
basin of beaten gold weighing two hundred and fifty
ounces, in the form of a peacock, "all whose tails was set
with diamonds, sapphires, rubies and other pearls of in-
estimable value."

Phipps, in his diary, tells of salvaging one hundred
and seventy tons of silver worth one million, four hundred and ninety pounds sterling. His men hoisted up
great hunks of coral and beat them open; in one piece
they found seven thousand, six hundred pieces of eight.
That was the equivalent of seven thousand, six hundred
dollars. It still is, for the piece of eight bits established
the value of our silver dollar. Two bits remains a quarter of a dollar, four bits a half.

The fact that interested the Links and us was that
Phipps, in his diary, complained that the wreck was so
overgrown with coral that his divers never were able to
break into "ye bellie of ye ship" where the greatest bulk
of the treasure was said to be stored. Most of it was silver that the *Golden Lion* was carrying from the Potosí
Mines in Peru. The mines were discovered in 1545 by an

Indian, Hualpo; a vein three hundred feet long and thirteen feet broad with "a great outcrop above the ground the height of a lance—half silver, and in part all silver with flukes projecting out from the level of the hill." From this mountain of silver more than six hundred million dollars' worth of silver was mined and exported to Spain in ships like the *Golden Lion* that sank on Silver Shoals.

Since the day of Phipps, many expeditions have been attracted to Silver Shoals. All fared badly. Thirty years ago Reisberg wrote how the evil spell of Silver Shoals almost cost him his leg. Verill found a platinum ingot but was shipwrecked. Later Craig's expedition was repelled by a hurricane. The Russian Kargenoff's ended in mutiny. Now it was our turn to explore the silver-cursed reef.

"Phipps' chart and ours agree," Link said, "the course is one hundred and sixty degrees on Seven Brothers light. We should get to the shoals at 10 o'clock tomorrow."

As Ed set the automatic pilot and arranged the watches, I felt the first twinges of uncertainty. The stars and the phosphorescent sparks in the bow waves seemed too bright, the air too soft, the sea too calm. After taking our turn at watch, Jane and I went to sleep in a cabin in the V of the bow where just forward of our bunks the anchor chains were piled. It was a peaceful night on a quiet sea. We hoped the good weather would last.

In the morning there was still a flat calm. Great

patches of golden-brown seaweed floated on the shiny, leaden sea. The deck was littered with foot-long flying fish that had flown aboard during the night. We trolled a jig for mackerel, but every one we hooked got bitten in two by a barracuda before we could get it to the boat.

At 10 o'clock I was in the crow's nest, forty feet above the deck, looking for the reef. Far ahead and to starboard there was a spout of white water, then another and another. At first I thought it was a school of whales, for how else could spouts of water rise from a flat and waveless sea? Then through the clear water ahead, I saw the coral of Silver Shoals, a flat-topped tower rising in water that the fathometer said was up to ninety feet deep. We slowed the motor and crept on, watching the spouts that Phipps in his diary had called "boilers."

The coral grew in skyscrapers, seventy to ninety feet tall, and spread out, a foot below the surface, to form flat roofs, sometimes ten feet, sometimes a hundred yards in diameter. Even on a dead calm day like this, the ground swells from the open ocean rolled in among the corals and broke as they hit the seaward edge of each flat-top. The breaking wave was slowed as it foamed across the surface, while the unbroken swells at the sides rolled on at their former speed. Then a strange thing happened: the water from the swell on the sides and from behind rushed in across the bare coral to fill the space ahead of the slowed and breaking wave so that four waves met in the center with a deep, water-shaking roar. The spray shot upward into a geyser twenty feet high.

"What would Silver Shoals be like in a storm?" I said to Kemp.

"We better not be here," the Bahamian said shortly.

Phipps' diary located the wreck "near where the reef was making like to a half moon." Close by, it said, was the "dry rock."

For an hour we threaded our way through the flat-topped corals. From the mast head we could see that far ahead the reef curved inward in a crescent bay. As we came close we saw a rock rearing up from the sluggish sea. It was the only rock above the water. It seemed to be the spot that Phipps had described. The question was where and how to anchor in this totally exposed and reef-filled stretch of sea.

The underwater plateau of Silver Shoals fell off abruptly into unfathomable depths in which it was impossible to anchor. On the plateau itself the water was from seventy to ninety feet deep, but everywhere were the massive coral flat-tops separated by deep water. The coral made it dangerous to anchor, for there was no area large enough to allow the *Sea Diver* to swing around on her mooring without hitting a coral head.

"We'll have to set a stern anchor too," Link said.

We anchored the *Sea Diver* fore and aft, Kemp carrying the anchors out in the dinghy and letting them down to the bottom between the coral heads. Then Jane and I went out in the dinghy to explore. At the "dry rock" we went overboard with face plates and flippers, into the clearest water we had ever seen. In this stagnant, nutrient-depleted eddy of the ocean's currents, plankton is so scarce that visibility under water is one hundred to two hundred feet. We could see every detail of the bottom eighty feet below, and up from this bottom rose the corals. Their craggy vertical walls mushroomed out near the surface in response to plankton and light.

Their flat "roofs" were a foot under water. We swam up to one of them, hung onto its overhanging edge and looked across the top. The sunlight on the gold and purple corals was dazzling. Everywhere in the intricacies of the formations were tiny fish as bright as the corals. Above them the silver ceiling of the water gently rose and bent and fell.

Below us, on the wall of the flat-top, a six-foot barracuda hung like a torpedo, ready to strike. Slowly it opened and shut its mouth, showing wolf-like teeth. Far below dark-skinned groupers gaped at us from shadowy caves.

On a sloping bank beside one of these coral formations we discovered scattered piles of coral-encrusted ballast stones, round granite stones from some old-world beach. They could have been a part of the wreck of the *Golden Lion* or of a sunken salvage vessel. I dived down, broke loose one of the smaller ballast stones and brought it up to the surface. We lifted it into the dinghy, left a buoy to mark the spot, and brought the stone back to the *Sea Diver*.

"There are only a few small piles of ballast," Jane told Ed, "not enough for a ship the size of the *Golden Lion.*"

"Maybe she was so full of silver she didn't need any

other ballast," Link said. "Let's see what else is down there."

We launched the *Reef Diver,* a small, jet-propelled powerboat that was stored on the *Sea Diver's* deck, and went back to the buoy to search. Nearby, Link found a huge, coral-crusted anchor, and scattered in the ballast stones we salvaged musket barrels, broken bottles, and a few silver coins, now changed to black masses of silver salts. There was no pattern of a shipwreck, though, no metallic silver and no gold.

Beside a knob of bright yellow coral Jane found a hole that led down into the reef. We poked into it with fishing rods and peered in with underwater flashlights.

"It's 'ye bellie of ye ship,'" Jane said, when she surfaced. "Let's dynamite it."

Link agreed. He set the charges and laid the wires. Everyone got out of the water and into the *Reef Diver* to avoid the blast. Link touched a wire to the battery. There was a snapping sound and a bump that made our boat rattle. Huge yellowish smoke-filled bubbles came to the top. Parrot fish, belly up, drifted by. We waited for the cloud of coral dust to settle, then Kemp and Vidal watched skeptically as the four of us went overboard to see what had happened. We found a hole six feet in diameter blown in the reef and at its bottom was a cave. It was empty—no artifacts, no bars of silver, no peacocks of gold.

"But they're there somewhere," Jane said when we came up to talk about it.

That night, thoughts of the coral heads haunted me.

They had not changed since Verill, shipwrecked on them half a century ago, wrote "of the sharp tartar-like corals endowed with some malignant purpose, terrible, sinister monsters of destruction that made even the most hardened of our men, old sailors that they were, confess to a feeling of terror." In the morning I felt no fear though, for we were busy diving in the warm, bright sea. The daytime water was clear, silent, sunny and familiar. Dangers could be seen and comprehended. It was after sunset when the water turned dark and mysterious that the terror was felt, as the reefs groaned and breathed up their threatening waves.

We spent ten days on Silver Shoals, moving ballast stones and salvaging artifacts from the wreck. All were disintegrated and scattered. Everything was overgrown with coral, so that the shapes were disguised.

Every night the wind blew a half gale. The sea came up and the boilers roared in the darkness. The *Sea Diver* pitched and rolled and timbers creaked. The anchor chains jerked and groaned. Jane and I were in the forward cabin, through which passed the anchor chains rattling and grinding as the ship pitched. I became afraid to sleep. If the anchors slipped or the ropes broke, we would be wrecked on the giant flat-tops. No planes passed this lonely reef. We were out of range of radio. We were "beyond the track of ships."

The worst thing about those nights was that there was nothing to do, no action to take to protect us from the constant threat of danger. If there had been something active going on, I might have been less tense.

I remembered a time a year before when Jane and I

had been in deadly danger and I had felt no fear. We had been fifty miles from land, on the Little Bahama Bank with the Links. They had taken the *Sea Diver* off to investigate a distant section of the reef and had left Jane and me to dive from the dinghy. We had been exploring the outer edge of a bank where the water was only ten feet deep, looking for wrecks, swimming and diving, towing the dinghy with a rope. For twenty miles around us there was no land, and there was no water less than ten feet deep. Suddenly we had seen that the bottom was covered with cannons. In our excitement we let the rope go, each thinking the other had it. Time after time we had dived, while the forgotten dinghy floated away with the wind and tide. When we finally looked up the dinghy was on the horizon, moving steadily off. I knew that two heads floating in a vast expanse of moving ocean would be hard to see.

I had set out after the dinghy knowing that an empty boat could drift swiftly in even a whisper of wind. In five minutes she had gone two hundred yards. If her drift had been all from wind, I could never have caught her. We had been in deadly danger, but as I started to swim I had had no feeling of fear. I was too busy. Luckily for us, the dinghy's drift had been largely from the tide. Within a quarter mile I swam her down.

Here on Silver Shoals it was different. There was danger and fear and nothing to do to remedy them or make me forget them. Every morning on the *Sea Diver* we repaired the damage of the night before. Once we found an anchor rope sawed nearly in two, held only by a strand. New links had to be welded to repair anchor chains ground thin on the coral. The moorings were fouled and their buoys were tangled. And all the time the boilers kept steaming and spouting like a heated pot.

Sometimes Ed would dive down ninety feet with his Desco mask and air hose to reset an anchor. I worried not only about him but about the rest of us if anything should happen to our navigator.

"I'll do it," Link always declared when someone else volunteered. "I have been trained in this sort of thing."

Each day, when all was repaired and in order, we set off on a silent sea. Each night, Jane and I tried to sleep in our chain-rattling forward cabin. We found ourselves up time after time with flashlights, checking anchors and mooring buoys. Sometimes we slept on deck at the stern, listening to the grunts of the boilers and the whistling of the wind. It was better than the grinding of the chains in the cabin.

I knew Ed to be an utterly nerveless creature who had spent his life facing danger in the air and under the sea. Marion had shared in many of his adventures and seemed as oblivious of danger as he. Kemp was a Bahamian, raised from a baby on these unpredictable waters. Vidal, like most Canadian guides I had known, was imperturbable. I observed Jane, too, and how she seemed totally unaware of our danger. I knew she had dealt with fear often, when she had been a pilot. I admired the lot of them, and felt I was the only one on Silver Shoals who was really afraid.

On the ninth night came the worst storm of all. In

the morning an anchor rope was broken, and the chain of another was badly worried by the coral. The sea was flat, the sun was small and silvery, and the sky was coppery. Huge ground swells rolled in from the Atlantic, and reared and broke on the flat-tops of the coral reef. Like monsters, they rose and foamed and disappeared.

We dived all day in the threatening water. In the evening Ed tried to get a weather report on the radio-telephone. He could not establish contact. I dreaded the night to come and the storm that I knew would accompany the darkness.

The wind started at midnight and by two o'clock was blowing harder than on any other night. Jane was restless ... In the middle of the gale's fury, she said, "Barney, I smell onions cooking."

I did too. "Who'd be cooking onions at this time of night?"

We went up to the galley. There was Marion at the stove over a steaming pan. She was turning the frying onions with a spoon.

"What are you making those for?" I asked.

Marion turned around. "I guess I just had to smell something familiar."

"You mean you're nervous?" Jane said.

"Aren't you, too?" Marion laughed.

"I've been scared to death for a week," Jane said.

I looked at them in astonishment. "I thought I was the only one who was!"

"Ed hasn't liked it either," Marion said.

By then Kemp and Vidal had joined us.

"We in a hurricane nest," Kemp said.

"Let's get out of here," Vidal suggested.

By this time Ed was there, too. "We'll leave in the morning," he told us, and we laughed in relief, for all of us had been afraid.

In the morning we raised anchors and left the boilers of Silver Shoals. "Let the gold and silver stay," Link said. "We might come back some other time."

We all agreed that we had done better than many of the crews that had worked the lonely reef. We had had no mutinies or panics. Of course, we had stayed on Silver Shoals only ten days. We thought of the courage of Phipps and his men in their primitive sailing ships and tiny boats spending nearly a year among these coral heads and boilers.

What makes courage and what makes fear? Unfamiliarity, uncertainty? At home, when a strange creature casts its shadow through the slats of our back yard fence, the mallards give shrieks of warning and fly squawking into the pond. The rabbit thumps a hind leg and heads for cover.

The unknown is apt to be the most fearsome. It breeds panic and morbid fear. And though, as yet, we had no indication of the threat that was to hang over us in coming years, both Jane and I had gained knowledge of the force of fear.

"We in a hurricane nest," Kemp said.

"Let's get out of here," Vidal suggested.

By this time Ed was there, too. "We'll leave in the morning," he told us, and we laughed in relief, for all of us had been afraid.

In the morning we raised anchors and left the boilers of Silver Shoals. "Let the gold and silver stay," Link said. "We might come back some other time."

We all agreed that we had done better than many of the crews that had worked the lonely reef. We had had no mutinies or panics. Of course, we had stayed on Silver Shoals only ten days. We thought of the courage of Phipps and his men in their primitive sailing ships and tiny boats spending nearly a year among these coral heads and boilers.

What makes courage and what makes fear? Unfamiliarity, uncertainty? At home, when a strange creature casts its shadow through the slats of our back yard fence, the mallards give shrieks of warning and fly squawking into the pond. The rabbit thumps a hind leg and heads for cover.

The unknown is apt to be the most fearsome. It breeds panic and morbid fear. And though, as yet, we had no indication of the threat that was to hang over us in coming years, both Jane and I had gained knowledge of the force of fear.

the morning an anchor rope was broken, and the chain of another was badly worried by the coral. The sea was flat, the sun was small and silvery, and the sky was coppery. Huge ground swells rolled in from the Atlantic, and reared and broke on the flat-tops of the coral reef. Like monsters, they rose and foamed and disappeared.

We dived all day in the threatening water. In the evening Ed tried to get a weather report on the radio-telephone. He could not establish contact. I dreaded the night to come and the storm that I knew would accompany the darkness.

The wind started at midnight and by two o'clock was blowing harder than on any other night. Jane was restless ... In the middle of the gale's fury, she said, "Barney, I smell onions cooking."

I did too. "Who'd be cooking onions at this time of night?"

We went up to the galley. There was Marion at the stove over a steaming pan. She was turning the frying onions with a spoon.

"What are you making those for?" I asked.

Marion turned around. "I guess I just had to smell something familiar."

"You mean you're nervous?" Jane said.

"Aren't you, too?" Marion laughed.

"I've been scared to death for a week," Jane said.

I looked at them in astonishment. "I thought I was the only one who was!"

"Ed hasn't liked it either," Marion said.

By then Kemp and Vidal had joined us.

At the same time, the campaign of public education was drawing heavily on the weapon of fear. This often had the opposite of the desired effect, for some people grew so afraid of cancer or its treatment that they refused to see a physician even when they had symptoms. I felt that there was need for a book to put cancer in a common-sense perspective, along with the other diseases that beset man. And so in 1955 I wrote a book on cancer, designed for the public to read.

The philosophy of the book is summarized in this excerpt from it:

> *The role of education is to point out that some things are indeed inevitable; to teach the importance of those things that are important; and to teach us to accept with dignity those facts of life that we cannot change.*

No sooner had the book been published than Jane was found to have a cancer.

Jane's reaction to the diagnosis was factual, positive, intellectual, but not devoid of emotion. On my pillow, on the evening of the day I had taken her to the hospital, I found a note.

> *Barney*
> *Like wings over waves*
> *Silent-timeless*
> *Love glides in ecstasy*
> ♡ *Jane*
> *December 5th 1959*

Four days after the operation Jane fulfilled a lecture engagement. Her reaction to her illness was typified in a letter to a friend:

> *. . . First of all let me tell you that I am now a statistic. An innocent-looking, minute lump turned out to be a cancer. It was in the so-called first stage. Supposedly I have an eighty percent chance of it not recurring, yet I must admit I feel a bit as I did one day on Ed Link's* Sea Diver *when he said, 'Be careful the way you sit down on that box, Jane, it has a hundred sticks of dynamite in it!'*
>
> *It is ironic that this should happen to Barney— yet perhaps fateful. Breast cancer is Barney's particular field—one of the most controversial, the least understood. Barney has been talking about, studying and thinking about growth in all its fascinating ramifications for a long time. Now this has turned the tide and he is going half time into research. Suddenly he has found a new world. I am valiantly trying to learn about deoxyribonucleic acids, D.N.A. and the magic of chemistry so that I will be able to recognize what language he is speaking.*

Jane had always helped me in the editing of my medical books and papers. She knew that the likelihood of cure was determined not so much by the size of the tumor as by its type. Small as Jane's had been, it was not of a good type. What the outcome would be, time alone would tell. In any event she wanted to understand as much about the disease as she could, and we decided that she would come to my laboratory three mornings a week to help in my cancer research. We were studying the growth and spread of cancers in mice and their control by surgery, radiation, and chemicals.

It is one thing to know what you want to study in a laboratory and another to learn how to study it. We knew that we wanted to study the effects of the body's lymphocytes and immune system on the growth and spread of cancers in mice. What we didn't know was how to catch mice loose in a laboratory.

The morning that Jane and I started work, a hundred and fifty mice were huddled in a yard-square wire cage, one side of which opened as a swinging door. Confidently, I opened the door and reached for a mouse. The colony exploded like popcorn. Mice by the dozens flew out of the open door and scattered throughout the room and building. The rest of the morning we spent in catching them, not without our share of mouse bites.

Gradually, we learned how to handle mice, transplant tumors, and study the factors that influenced growth and metastasis, or spread, of cancers. The most important thing that I learned was that the director of a research program must know how to do the things his technicians do or at least must know exactly how they do it. Experiments cannot be done by remote control. It is only by seeing the results that an investigator gets the feeling of their significance. It is only by doing the work oneself or by watching a technician do it that the need for controls at every stage is appreciated.

Jane, in addition to helping with the technical work, was my laboratory accountant. Often we handled as many as four hundred new mice a week and had as many as fifteen hundred in the laboratory, jumping out of cages, getting into wrong cages, dying, getting eaten by one another, and sometimes, even in an "all-female" colony, reproducing. The task of setting up a system to account for each of these mercurial units was staggering. It was not until Jane sternly demanded an accurate account of each mouse that I appreciated the full extent of human error, chiefly my own. But eventually our experiments began to take form and we had the satisfaction of transferring some of the information we had gained into clinical practice with patients.

Although our daily life went on generally as it always had, Jane's illness made both of us conscious of the uncertainty of our future. We sensed the preciousness of time. Suddenly it had become compressed and finite. Life had to be fitted into a smaller package.

There were things we had always wanted to do together, places we wanted to visit. We had already seen much of the Western world, Europe, and the Americas. We felt the urge to go to the Middle East, to the ancient lands of Palestine. We decided to visit the Byzantine Empire, and to follow the routes that the Crusaders marched. We wanted to learn something of the Arabs and the Moslem way of life.

And so in the summer of 1960 we flew to Jordan with George, Susie, and Ann. Joan was now married to a doctor who was going into surgery. Ann was on the

verge of marrying his roommate, another potential surgeon. Susie was a radiant seventeen, ready for college,
and George, at fifteen, was president of his class and
prominent in athletics. We left the three children with
friends in Jerusalem, and Jane and I set out for Petra,
which has been called the "rose red city half as
old as time." It had been a lost city until 1812, when
an archeologist from Switzerland, Johann Burck-
hardt, embraced the Moslem faith, lived with the nomadic Bedouins and learned the secrets of their lands.

It took us fourteen hours to drive to Petra. We followed the King's Highway. Our Arab driver, Kayad
Biter, drove at top speed around hairpin turns on the
rough dirt roads of Jordan's brutal mountains, which
rolled ahead of us into the horizon in a barren monotone
of tan.

The King's Highway was built on an ancient caravan route from Damascus to Arabia, heavily traveled
since the days of Moses. After Joseph was sold to
Potiphar, it was over this route that his caravan traveled. Armies of Greeks, Romans, Byzantines, and Crusaders have swarmed across it. Along this road came
camel caravans from the Aegean, from Arabia, Africa,
the Orient; trading spices, ivory, and silks. Through the
centuries the desert paths of the Middle East have remained the same. Along them rose and fell the great
cities: Babylon, Nineveh, Memphis, Ur, Petra. Upon the
harsh, dry plains that we were crossing, artificial
mounds, or "tels," marked the ruins of ancient civilizations, the mud and stone and potsherds of one city

heaped upon another. We had read of this and now were in the reality.

We passed through the still-inhabited village of Er Rabbah, which Deuteronomy says was originally inhabited by a race of giants. There King Og slept in a bed of iron thirteen and a half feet long. Jane pointed to a giant Arab standing at a lonely column on the plain.

For several hours we drove across the vast desert. We saw no one. Then ahead, at the top of a high ridge, loomed the turreted fortress of Kurak, which the Crusaders built at the site of Moab of the Bible.

We stopped before Kurak and as we walked up to its massive walls we wondered what motivated the Crusaders to leave their homes in Europe and travel thousands of miles across sea and wastelands to build a castle like this on a desert plain.

There seems to be a cyclic restlessness in man that, like the migratory instincts of animals and insects, impels him to move. The persistence of this instinct is expressed also in the chemistry of the body. In spring and fall there are many more recurrences of ulcers and flare-ups of chronic diseases than in summer or winter months. At the change of seasons, man's body undergoes some basic adaptation to change.

Besides this seasonal restlessness there is a mysterious tide that builds up within each generation, an unrestrainable urge to move. The lemmings have this "generational restlessness"; rats on occasion have banded together in hordes and swept over the countryside; locusts rise into the air aimlessly beating their wings, while the wind blows the swarm across the fields. Man, since the beginning of history, periodically sets out in armies like the Crusaders' to exploit an idea or conquer a world. Perhaps his purpose is as vague as the locusts', and he simply is impelled to move, then drifts in the direction of prevailing thought.

The Middle East at the time of the Crusades was partly Christian. It belonged to the Roman Empire, whose civilization has never died. In time the Empire split, and Constantinople became more powerful than Rome. From her, Christianity spread through the Middle East, where Christians lived in some harmony with Mohammedans. The Crusaders, a migration of over half a million restless people, marched into this complex of cultures. In Kurak, genetic evidence remained. We saw blue-eyed children with blond hair, and we were arrested by an Arab officer who looked like a Chevalier of France.

We were photographing the massive ruins of the fortress of the Crusaders when a captain in the British-trained army of Hussein's Hashemite Kingdom asked us for our passports. We had left them in Jerusalem. The officer, whose name, our driver told us, was Captain Sadi Taka, had a close-clipped moustache, white, even teeth, and a dimple in his chin. He wore a silver-buttoned, khaki uniform with an embossed, silver-buckled Sam Browne belt. When we told him, through our driver-interpreter, that we did not have our passports, he looked grave.

"The captain wishes you to accompany him to the

station," our driver interpreted. We followed the officer
through the courtyard into the castle, thinking of the
dungeons that must lie below.

We did not speak a word of Arabic and none of the
Arabs in the station spoke English or French. We had
no phrase book or dictionary. Our driver had been told
to remain in the car, and we had been hustled away
from him and into the fort before any explanations
could be made. Actually, none were possible, for we had
simply forgotten our passports and left them in our baggage. We tried without success to explain this. Captain
Taka motioned us to be seated in two of the chairs along
the walls of the square empty room. Two officers, armed
with pistols, came to sit opposite us, smoking, idly talking, and staring at us from time to time. An armed
guard stood at the door. Then Captain Taka said something and the guard disappeared. For half an hour Jane
and I sat on one side of the room, the officers on the
other. The men had fallen silent, and looked sober. We
too sat quietly, wordlessly looking out through a slit between blocks of stone to the rolling plains of Edom,
where the red and hairy Esau wandered after he traded
his birthright for that mess of pottage. We thought of
our birthrights, secure in our luggage in the Jerusalem
hotel.

The guard returned, this time without rifle and carrying a tray with six tiny porcelain coffee cups and a
shiny brass coffeepot. He passed us each a cup, filling it
with the strong, bitter Arab coffee. There was only a sin-

gle swallow in a cup. With a flourish of the copper pot
the attendant filled them again. We drank.

"Remember," Jane cautioned, "their custom is to
drink three times." We did. Then I waved a finger to indicate enough. The officers were pleased that we followed the tradition. We smiled. The atmosphere seemed
more friendly.

There were no words that we and the Arabs had in
common, except for modern ones like *telephone* or *camera,* and yet, warmed by the coffee, and an hour later by
sweetened tea served in the same way, we were able to
establish a kind of communication. We gleaned that we
were being held until a telephone message got through
to Jerusalem and clearance was obtained to let us pass
without our papers.

Captain Taka now suggested that he show us
through the ruins. He explained with gestures the significance of the Crusaders' carvings and the purpose of
the immense fortification. And then the telephone message came through. Safeguarded with a paper signed by
our Captain Taka, we waved goodbye and were in our
car and on the road to Petra once more.

The mountains rolled endlessly. In this wasteland,
fifty thousand nomadic Bedouins drove their flocks in a
never-ceasing search for water and grass. In a valley we
came to an oasis with palm trees, masses of shrubbery,
and pink blossoming oleanders. The oasis was the meeting place of the desert. The water belonged to all. An
Arab woman in black stood against the cliff, carding

wool. Her flock of black goats bounded down the embankment to join the ones drinking from the bubbling spring. In one hand she held a distaff with a mass of goat hair hanging, in the other a spindle weighted with a stone.

Resting at the oasis, too, were a pair of Arab landowners, Ahmed Motleg and Mohammed Kafir. The latter was six feet tall, bronzed, and in khaki shirt and pants. On his head he wore the Arab headdress, a white cotton kafia with a black ladder design in it and a braided black cord around the crown. The kafia, cool and comfortable, could be worn at different angles to signify various emotions from peace to war. Mohammed's was at a reassuringly neutral angle. Over an open fire by the well he had made a pot of tea. He asked Ahmed and us to share it with him.

Carrying the blackened copper teapot and china cups he led us over a stone wall into a jungle of fig trees, date palms, apricot and pomegranate trees. From thick vines hung branches of large, white grapes. He invited us to sit on a rounded, white limestone rock. It was like one we had just seen in Jerusalem from which Mohammed ascended to heaven. We sipped the tea, sweet like Captain Taka's but flavored with herbs and wild mint. We ate the ripe, warm grapes that he invited us to pick. The Garden of Eden, which is said to have been only a few miles away on the Syrian-Lebanese border, must have been no more pleasant and luxurious than this fragrant, fruit-laden pool of shade.

Ahmed Motleg was also in khaki and Arab head-

dress. He was older than Mohammed, carried a walking
stick and wore a big knife at his belt. In his breast
pocket were two pencils and a pen. He came with us in
the car and told us that although he was a landowner he
could not make a living from the land alone and was
also a supervisor of the men who worked on the roads.
He lived near the military post at Wadi Musa, where we
were to pick up horses to ride the last few miles into
Petra. At twilight we said goodbye to Ahmed on the terraced hillside near his house. He stood there a moment,
an impressive figure pointing with his stick over the deserted valley that once was the heart of the Nabataean
civilization. Below was the oasis, Moses' spring, from
which water for the great city of Petra had once been
piped.

Two thousand years ago, Petra, mentioned in the
Bible as "Sela, the rock," was the desert caravans' main
trading post. As we drove on down the winding road and
across the rocky mountainside, dark shadows from the
setting sun fell across the slopes. At the bottom of the
hill was the post, Wadi Musa, that guards the entrance
to Petra three miles away. It was a square, one-story
barracks for a couple of officers and a half a dozen men.
The captain who greeted us spoke good English.

"Spend the night here. We have beds for all of you.
It will be safer to go in by daylight."

Our time was short. We were to return to Jerusalem and meet our children there the next night.

"What is dangerous about going in at night?" we
protested.

"It is the young Israelis," the officer said. "They come over from the Negev and fight with our guards. They kill anyone they see."

"Nevertheless we have to go in tonight," Jane said.

"And we want to take pictures of Petra in the early morning sun," I backed her up firmly.

The officer looked at the pink clouds of sunset over the mountains, shrugging his shoulders as if clearing himself of responsibility. He said, "Then I will get you a guide." He turned to speak in Arabic to a boy who ran off.

He said to us, "While the guide is coming, may I give you a cup of tea?" He took us to his quarters.

Soon the guide, Abdul, came carrying a lantern and an ancient rifle. With him were two little Arab boys, Moses and Oselman, leading three pint-sized, sharp-backed horses without saddles or bridles. My horse, Isa, had a foal that ran beside her and nursed whenever she stopped. The little boys trotted alongside too.

The path to Petra went winding down the steep slopes of a valley, along a dry stream bed and across a rock-strewn plain. Great wind-carved, skull-like boulders grinned down on us. Ahead was a range of mountains a thousand feet high through which we saw no pass. That was why for ten centuries Petra lived only as a legend.

As we approached the mountains, Petra's secret was revealed: a cleft in the rock. It was the "Siq," said to have been made by Moses with a blow of his rod. It actually was formed by the ancient stream, now dry, whose bed we had followed. Its floods had cut the soft sandstone like a knife. The siq was three hundred feet deep and so narrow that in places we could touch both its vertical walls at the same time. It was dusk now. Abdul stopped his horse, lit his lantern, and loaded his rifle. Then he mounted again and rode on, the lantern casting gargantuan moving shadows on the stone. The boy, Moses, who was leading Jane's horse, was muttering to himself.

"What is he saying?" Jane asked Abdul.

"He prays that the Israelis will not come tonight."

For a mile and a quarter we rode through the mountain cleft, a ribbon of starlight lighting us from above and the red glow of the lantern guiding our horses' hoofs. Ten feet from the floor of the siq, a groove was carved in the solid rock wall and in it were fragments of Nabataean tile, once used to pipe water to Petra from Moses' spring.

The siq ended in a keyhole slit overhung by stone. Single file, our horses stepped through. Before us spread a deep canyon a hundred yards wide. In its wall, carved into the rock, loomed a great temple, ghostly in the starlight, its columns bigger than the Parthenon's, its façade ninety feet high. We stopped, just as through the centuries all visitors to Petra must have stopped. Only the foal was unimpressed. It began again to suckle.

We followed the gorge, the high walls giving back hollow echoes to the clicking of the horses' hoofs. In this solitary canyon were some of the most colossal ruins of ancient times. It was hard to tell in the starlight which of the sculptures had been formed by centuries of wind and water and which fashioned by man, ghosts of Nabataean labor.

After a five-minute ride the gorge widened and we found ourselves on a vast plain. Ahead on a high hillside was the glow of a camp fire. Our guide gave a long, high, haunting call, and through the darkness echoed an answer. It was from the Arab guard, Abdul told us.

We rode across the dimly starlit plain, past ruins and mounds that marked the graves of ancient buildings. Our horses' hoofs clattered on the flagging of a Roman road. A herd of goats bleated in the darkness. Further along, the Bedouin goatherd spoke to us softly as we went by.

We followed the Arab post's firelight across the ghostly valley. The guardsman swung a lantern. We dismounted at the foot of the hill and left the boys tethering the horses to the columns of a Roman ruin. Abdul led us up a trail on one side of the cliff to the Arab camp. The guard was standing alert with his musket cocked. When he recognized Abdul, he put his gun down and greeted us. He was Abu Aly Twassey, wrinkled and white-moustached, the deep furrows of his face accentuated by the fire and lantern light. He wore a tan tweed coat that draped nearly to his knees; a big knife hung in a silver-studded sheath, and he had on a black and white kafia. He picked up a black pot that was standing by the fire and offered us coffee.

We sat for a long time on the ledge of the cliff, sip-

ping the coffee and looking out over the waterless wasteland that had been chosen in the days of the Nabataeans
as the site of one of the greatest cities of ancient times.
Scientists have not recorded any great climatic changes
since the days of the Nabataeans. The amount of effort
required to bring water through the tiled aqueducts cut
in the walls of the siq was almost beyond our comprehension.

After coffee it was bedtime and the guard, Abu,
with eloquent gestures, offered us his bed—a ragged,
lumpy mattress, covered with a horse blanket. We accepted with thanks, grateful not to be on the floor of the
cliffside cave with the rock-rabbits.

We woke at dawn. Below, the desert was like an
opal, cool, luminous, and filled with color and change.
We could see the ruins of the palace of King Aretas IV,
whose daughter married Herod Antipas—the same
King Herod, who, the Bible relates, was so pleased by the
dancing of Salome that he promised to give her whatso-
ever she asked and redeemed his promise with John the
Baptist's head. And there were the ruins of a Roman
market place with rows of broken columns, scattered
bits of sculpture, and broken stones. Smooth mounds of
earth rose from the plain here and there, all that was
left of great buildings, buried with the passage of time.
We breakfasted on coffee, watermelon, and canned
beans, then set off to see the city of the dead.

In the ruins of Petra's Roman-period market place,
a dusky Bedouin woman came up to us, a black veil held
over her mouth. Her cheeks were blue with tattoos, her

eyes wide and like a deer's. She was, Abdul told us, one of the many Bedouins who made their living illegally by seeking out and plundering the ancient Nabataean graves. She had for sale Roman lamps, perfume bottles, and dozens of Roman coins. We bargained for them and bought a few.

Petra was not a concentrated monument, not a compact ruin, but a vast area extending for miles in every direction, up canyons and mountainsides whose soft pink sandstone had been carved into sculptured façades and filled with tombs and caves. When the sun rose over the cliffs and the bright light bathed the colored stone, its multicolored layers of sand rippled with waves of pink, rose, red, purple, yellow, and greenish-blue.

The significance of the colossal carvings at Petra, whether they were once temples or palaces or tombs, is unknown. They had classical façades whose columns were larger than any solid stone columns in the world. Roofs were carved in Grecian style. All of this had been wrought inexplicably by hammer and chisel in native stone.

At high noon, in the full heat of the day, we were about to leave Petra through the siq, when we passed a veiled woman dressed all in black. She was carrying a child and a heavy, cloth-wrapped bundle. As we approached, she put down her burden for a rest. We asked our guide where the woman was going. He spoke to her for a moment, then shrugged in a gesture of futility.

"She is a Bedouin," he said. "Yesterday her husband spoke the final words, 'Woman, I thee divorce.' Now she must return to her family with her belongings and her child."

With a submissive, resigned air, the woman picked up her bundle and her baby and set off again through the siq to the desert beyond.

The code of the Moslem world was not everywhere as rigid as amongst the Bedouins. Earlier, Jane and I had visited Damascus, where a sea of desert made an island city that had endured for three thousand years. It was the oldest inhabited city on earth. The "street called straight" mentioned in the Bible, and the spice shops in the covered bazaar, stood just as they did when St. Paul walked the market place. Through the centuries the ways of the Arab merchants had shown little change. There were still the hundreds of competitive shops, each selling the same wares, each crowded into a little stall with a living space behind it where the family slept and ate. Women did not stray from this narrow domain; family ties were strong; children were cherished. The laws of hospitality were obeyed. There was enough to eat. Generation after generation, the conventional gracious Arab way of life still went on.

As Jane and I watched the Bedouin woman and her baby cross the desert, we thought of some of our friends at home. Many of them had experienced great unhappiness in the arrangement of their lives and loves. Often it seemed they were trying to do things that they were not adapted to do well, and that they were pretending to be things they were not. Perhaps, when a way of life is taught to children, it should not be too rigidly insisted upon. Alternative ways of living could also be taught. Perhaps there is too much emphasis on teaching "the truth," for truth is always changing. If children were brought up to believe that truth was not absolute, but an interpretation of things as we see them at a given time, there might be less friction in the world, more tolerance and contentment.

As we rode back through the siq, we were not certain that there was any more happiness in the rigidity of our Western culture than in that of the Middle East. In a day we would cross the border of Jordan into Israel and there see another ancient culture, this one newly set in place and time.

7

A STEP
THROUGH TIME—
PALESTINE, 1960

And God fulfills himself in many ways
Lest one good custom should corrupt the world.

—Tennyson

When we got back to Jerusalem we picked up Ann, Susie and George, who had stayed with friends there. The next day we all walked across the border into Israel, carrying our luggage, through the Mandelbaum Gate.

The transition from Jerusalem, Jordan, to Jerusalem, Israel, is only a step in space but it is century in time. On one side is the old, slow-moving Arab world, on the other the bustle of a modern city. We rented a car in Jerusalem and set off for Haifa where we planned to join the Links on the *Sea Diver*.

As we entered the countryside Jane and I were reminded of a spot in our back yard called "the weed patch." We fenced it in by wire against the nibblings of our rabbit and goose. We never planted anything in it, but kept it fertilized with wood mold. It was the most luxuriant part of the garden, one weed outgrowing another so that it changed continually, even from month to month.

Before we fenced in "the weed patch," the rabbit and goose had kept it eaten and trodden bare. It was like those desert hills of Jordan where man had cut the trees and goats consumed the vegetation. Here in Israel we found millions of pines, planted during the British mandate, making the goat-banned hillsides as green as the forests of Canada.

Israel was a mixture of old and new in a stage of transition. In Nazareth, still predominantly an Arab town, we saw girls, as in Biblical days, carrying jars of water from the well. A donkey, like the one that Mary rode, stood outside one of the carpenter shops on the narrow cobbled street where Jesus worked. And we drank the cold clear water from Mary's well. Then we visited the Weizmann Institute, one of the world's finest institutions of fundamental research on everything from atomic energy to the biological sciences.

The Links, since we had sailed with them to Silver Shoals, had built a new *Sea Diver,* twenty-five feet longer than the old one. She was a ninety-foot sea-going salvage vessel equipped with whatever was needed for underwater research and diving. The aim of the Link

Expedition, in collaboration with the Princeton Theological Seminary and the America-Israel Society, was to examine the underwater ruins of Caesarea, built by Herod the Great in 10 B.C., in its day the greatest port of the Mediterranean.

At Haifa we found the *Sea Diver* temporarily out of commission, docked for repairs. Heavy surges and rough, rolling seas off Caesarea had snapped her lines, torn her bumpers, and banged her sides against the remnants of an Arab seawall. The Links had taken the little jet-propelled *Reef Diver* overland to the Sea of Galilee to see what lay on the bottom there. The only thing our family could do at Caesarea was to dive from the shore and map out the sunken buildings for the Links, so that when the *Sea Diver* was repaired they would have a head start on their research.

Caesarea was on the coast, half a mile off the main road, between Haifa and Tel Aviv. We reached it by a narrow dusty lane that crossed the coastal plain, lush with banana trees, vineyards and gardens of legumes. This was land reclaimed from desert by the people of Sedot Yam, the village where we were going to stay. The countryside looked like any other cultivated area but suddenly, near Caesarea, in the middle of a tilled field, there was a fragment of an aqueduct, an excavated temple, and a Roman racetrack. Everywhere the ground was littered with potsherds—fragments of ancient pottery and pieces of tiles. Two thousand years ago this was a vast city of half a million. Pontius Pilate lived here; St. Paul was imprisoned here; and here the green-crystal Chalice was found, the "Holy Grail," now in Genoa, that is believed to be the cup used by Jesus at the Last Supper.

Above the ground there was nothing to be seen of the Roman city, but standing on its buried ruins were the remains of a walled citadel built by the Crusaders, and on top of those ruins medieval Arab buildings. Caesarea had been deserted since the thirteenth century when conquering Arabs smashed the aqueducts and the escaping water made a malarial swamp of the plain.

We climbed to the top of the ruins and looked out over the windswept harbor, wondering what had become of the huge mole, the towers, lighthouses, palaces, and colossal statues that the historian Flavius Josephus described. Now the waves pounded in on a deserted beach of sand. A small modern mole was crumbling into the sea. Lying in the shallows like wind-fallen logs were dozens of granite pillars that had supported a classical temple.

We drove past the ruins and along the coast for a quarter of a mile, then parked at a drawgate that blocked the road. Behind it were the buildings of Sedot Yam. We ducked under the gate and walked down a tree-shaded street looking for someone to direct us to the Links' friend, Mr. Wegman, an archeologist who had arranged rooms for us. A group of suntanned Israeli-born children—"Sabras," they are called, named for the fruit of the cactus, hard and prickly outside but soft and warm within—were striding down the street talking and laughing, girls in shorts and white shirts, and boys in blue jeans and blue work shirts. We asked them how to find Mr. Wegman. They shrugged their shoulders, gestured indifferently that they did not speak English and walked on. We had felt the Sabras' prickles and had not yet touched the fruit within.

At the post office we learned where Wegman was and went to find him at the site of his archeological dig in the old Crusader Moat. He was tall and taut-muscled, with a strong, sensitive, suntanned face. He descended from the top of the wall and greeted us all in the Hebrew way, "Shalom, Shalom"—Peace be with you.

Wegman returned with us to show us our house. On the way we passed a pink-stucco dining-hall building and many whitewashed, tile-roofed houses, bright with flowers. Our house was the last one of the settlement, two rooms on the edge of the desert. Beyond it was barren salty land. Our neighbor, who lived in a house just like ours, was reclaiming his back yard from the desert by putting wheelbarrowsful of top soil over the sand and then sprinkling to get rid of the salt. Next year he too would have a garden.

In our house we had a washbasin, shower and toilet, and in each room were two chairs, a table, two daybeds, a chest, a built-in bookcase and an electric light hanging from a cord. This was the typical living space of the kibbutz, Wegman told us. From this point on, a couple could decorate or furnish as they wished.

After we were settled, Wegman invited us to his house for coffee. On the way we stopped at the kibbutz' museum, a bright, airy two-room building a little larger than our house. Here were displayed capitals of marble columns, fragments of statues, lamps, glassware, coral-crusted amphoras that fishermen had raised in their nets, a collection of artifacts, jewelry and seals, and more than four thousand coins that had been picked up in the fields or on the shore. All of this had been found by accident, because formal excavations had just been started.

Wegman's house was shaded by bamboo and euca-lyptus trees and surrounded by a green lawn on which stood the marble capitals of three Corinthian columns supporting slabs of marble to make tables in the shade. Over our coffee he told us that the idea of the kibbutz, or communal settlement, began with a forty-eight-year-old Russian Jew obsessed with the idea that "if we do not till the soil with our own hands, it will not be ours." In 1911 he brought ten boys and two girls to the Jordan Valley near the Sea of Galilee and started the first kib-butz, Degania. There was to be equality for all—women to be equal to men, everyone to work with his hands, no private property, and no money. The land was to be rented from a national fund and held in the name of the people.

Now, Wegman said, there were nearly three hundred kibbutzim, some with as many as fifteen hundred mem-bers, as well as other types of collective settlements. Many of the kibbutzim had expanded into industry and ran factories, canneries, and even ocean-going freight-ers. There was a central banking system, but agriculture and reclaiming the desert were still the main business of the kibbutzim.

Sedot Yam had a population of six hundred. Communal life started in the crib, Wegman told us, for all the babies lived in one house and were taken care of by nurses so that both parents could work. Older children lived together, ate together, and visited with their parents only in late afternoon and evening. The kibbutz supplied the people with what they needed.

"But what if a child has some special talent?" Jane asked Wegman.

"He won't be neglected," Wegman told her. "The needs of the child are discussed by the committee, and if the child shows real talent, he'll be helped to cultivate it. We just bought a good violin for a musical girl, sent a boy to a university for advanced training in biology, and sent another abroad for study."

Wegman went on to explain that at eighteen both boys and girls went into the Army for two years. Although they had free choice of where to go afterward, ninety per cent of them elected to return to the kibbutz.

"Where can we go to look for coins?" George, treasure-hungry, asked Wegman.

"If you want to look on land," Wegman said, "you can go anywhere, for there are coins and seals and lamps lying all over the fields. A doctor and his wife come here every Saturday to find coins. They stand in the fields, look carefully, then take a step and look again. In fifteen years, they've found over a thousand coins with clear markings."

"What about the underwater part of the city?" Ann, our best swimmer, asked.

"No one knows how much of the city is underwater,"

Wegman said, "but there's a lot of it. When the water's clear, you can see the old Roman mole that once protected the harbor."

We had finished our coffee and it was still only mid-afternoon. "Let's take a look at that harbor," Jane said, intent.

We invited Wegman to come but he said he had to go back to the excavation. With face plates and flippers, the rest of us set out for the beach.

Jane and I had dived on shipwrecks and sunken cities and on romantic ruins from Mexico to the Mediterranean, but we had never learned to bridle our imaginations. In spite of many years of disillusionment, we still believed each new venture would lead us to the kind of wrecks or ruins that we would like to see. Not even the five-foot breakers rolling into the muddy harbor of Caesarea discouraged us. We were sure we would go right to the ruins of Herod's palace and find his throne and treasures of gold. The children, however, decided to search on land.

Jane and I waded out from the beach into cold, opaque water, fouled by the silt of Wegman's excavations, and then swam seaward. From time to time we dived and groped around on the flat, sandy bottom. For one hundred and fifty yards we swam out, finding nothing. Then the water began to clear. It was fifteen feet deep with a visibility of ten feet. I dived to the bottom and there, half buried in sand, was an enormous block of stone.

For the next hour Jane and I dived continually,

trying to make out what it was that we had found. There were massive square and oblong blocks of granite and columns lying one on top of another. The columns were thirty feet long, round, and so large that our arms could go only a third of the way around them. We scraped the slime off and uncovered rough pink stone, like the granite of the ruins of Balbec that twenty centuries ago had been quarried at Aswan, on the upper Nile. These were the remains of a huge building made of the best available material.

We were shivering with cold as we swam shoreward. Fifty yards from the beach Jane dived down and found the stock of a ten-foot iron anchor. It was older than the nineteenth century, with no cross-piece, just a hole for a bar of wood. We marked it by triangulation, lining up landmarks in two directions, and went ashore.

A young man who had been watching us introduced himself. He was Daniel Berman, a geophysicist and underwater geologist from the Hebrew University, who had been studying the fossils on the coastline to find out how much the land had sunk. We told him what we had discovered.

"In the last twenty centuries the land has settled fifteen feet," he said. "That's why the building you found out there is so far under water."

Berman said there were many theories as to why the coast was sinking, but the one he favored was that it was being sunk by the weight of the silt from the Nile. Silt from Ethiopia had raised the level of the valley of the Nile seven feet since the days of Cleopatra. It was silt from the flooding Nile as much as dirt from Wegman's excavations that made the water off this coast so turbid.

"In another two thousand years," Berman said, "Israel may lose a great deal of its flat and fertile coastal plain to the sea."

Everywhere on the beach was evidence of inexorable change. Lying in the shallows were walls built with great blocks of stone in the Herodian style, bits of marble, piles of broken pottery and tiles. Above the beach was a storm-washed cliff fifteen feet high. From top to bottom the cliff was studded with fragments of pottery, pieces of pink tile and bits of ancient glass. It was there we came upon the children, excavating the cliffside. We joined them and, digging together, soon found a Roman seal and two coins. Already the children had collected a dozen such relics. The cliff was a cross section of history spanning twenty centuries, a sea-made archeological excavation that we could mine, looking for the telltale green of ancient brass and dreaming of the glint of gold.

For a week Jane, the children, and I stayed at Sedot Yam, diving in the ruins of Caesarea and prospecting in its crumbling soil. We slipped and lost our footing on the cliffside, setting off avalanches of shale and clay. We were inundated by clouds of dust and dirt. A ray of sunshine would strike a bit of brass, arsenical green, or glint on ancient glass shimmering like an opal. There would be a shout. Someone had found a copper coin, an Arab ring or a sapphire-blue glass bottle stopper or bottom of a hanging lamp. There was something hypnotic about digging in that cliff. The next find might be an Arab jewel. It was never dull, for always there were graceful handles or pointed bottoms of amphora or bits of broken lamps.

When we first came to Sedot Yam, the kibbutzniks had been cool and seemed almost suspicious of us, but as the days passed their attitudes changed. All of us came back tired and dirty from our excavations. Ann and Susie worked with the girls of the kibbutz picking grapes. George, one night, proved himself to be a champion athlete in a game of skill and balance in which the opponents try to knock one another off of tippy chairs. We had been accepted by the community; we felt its warmth.

There seemed to be no real differences in the attitudes of the young people that we had met in Israel, whether they lived in communal kibbutzim or in free-enterprise cities in Haifa. In each system were well-adjusted, hard-working people who liked what they were doing and were happy with the opportunities they had found. In each, there were disgruntled people who did not like their jobs. Neither communal living nor private enterprise filled the dreams and aspirations of everyone. Because each person differs from every other, there always will be room for more than a single way of life.

The Negev Desert is Israel's great frontier, and it was there that new kibbutzim were constantly being formed to accommodate new immigrants to Israel. After leaving Caesarea, we flew over the Negev from Tel Aviv to the Red Sea and looked down onto ghostly ruins of forgotten civilizations choked with the desert's sand. Here and there were new kibbutzim, little clumps of houses surrounded by irrigated patches of green. There were military bases, too, for the Negev lies between less than two million Israelis and their twenty-five million enemies in Egypt.

After an hour-and-a-half flight we landed in Eilat, Israel's port on the Gulf of Aqaba. Land transport across the Negev to the Gulf and the Red Sea bypasses the Arab-held Suez Canal and gives Israel access to Africa and the East. In four years, Eilat had grown from a military outpost to a town of over six thousand. It had a frontier-sort of society with seven hundred bachelors and only twenty-five unmarried girls, at least so the travel guide advertised.

As we got off the plane, the hot wind from the Negev struck us like a blast. It was one hundred and fifteen degrees in the shade but so dry that sweat evaporated immediately. The blue sea in front of our hotel looked invitingly cool.

The sun was slanting down over the mountains when we waded from the burning-sand beach into the water of that same sea that once opened for the wandering tribes of Israel. To our astonishment it was icy. The Red Sea is over seven thousand feet deep, a part of the crack in the earth's crust that starts in Tanganyika, Africa, and forms the Great Rift Valley, the Red Sea, the Jordan Valley, and the Dead Sea. From the frigid depths of this rift came the water that lapped the Red Sea's hot beaches. With face plates and flippers we dived in.

Jane and I had never before in all our diving seen water like this. It was clear as air, with visibility we estimated at over two hundred feet. Its color was sapphire blue, the bubbles bright silver in the sunlight. Each detail of the bottom was clear. Entranced, all of us snorkeled along, dodging ghostly jellyfish that pulsed by trailing pale tentacles through the blue. There were no corals here and few fish. As the sun set behind the mountains, we came ashore.

Some say it was the red sunsets reflected from the hills that gave the sea its name. The evening was cool and when the sun went down, there were bright stars and the lights of ships anchored in the harbor of Eilat and off Jordan's Aqaba, a mile across the bay. We planned next morning to see the famous Red Sea coral that grew luxuriantly five miles up the coast near the Egyptian border.

We have sometimes noticed, when diving far at sea on lonely reefs, that suddenly for no apparent reason, the water will either cloud or clear. Perhaps it is plankton, eggs or sperm of fish, or clouds of microscopic animals that come in like haze and then vanish again into the pelagic stream. Although there had been no wind during the night at Eilat, the water in the morning had lost the sapphire quality of the evening before. It was clear, but no longer blue, and had the cold, white light of a diamond.

As we swam out from the sandy beach, we came to reefs of coral ten feet high—bright orange, blue, green, and gold. The fish were much like those of the Caribbean; butterfly fish with make-believe eyes in the markings of their tails, azure and gold angelfish, parrot fish nibbling at the coral with bird-like beaks, long-billed transparent needlefish, moray eels with gaping mouths, groupers fanning themselves sullenly under the ledges, and a myriad of tiny orange fishlets hanging like jewels in the mouths of the caves.

We found an eight-foot octopus under an old piece of iron, and chased him through his ink cloud until he disappeared into a cave. There were scorpion fish, lying camouflaged on the bottom, ready to sting. There were strange "sea snakes" that were not snakes at all—creatures six feet long and an inch in diameter that were a type of anemone with a Medusa's circle of snakelets around the mouth and nothing but an empty skin behind. There were sea cucumbers, eighteen inches long, that vomited out their guts when we picked them up. The guts stuck to us like chewing gum when we touched them and we couldn't get them off. They would grow another set. Then there were lion fish—dozens of them, varying from babies six inches long, to huge, sharp-quilled creatures that hung in the coral caves, covered with bright-colored poisonous spines. If you bump into a lion fish, which you can easily do for they are quite unafraid, their sting is sometimes fatal. It was a rich and frightening sea, with the coral reef shelving steeply into the abyss, and the salinity supporting us high in the water as we drifted along the edge.

When we had parked our car at the checkpoint of the Egyptian border, we had made sure that we swam in the right direction. The guards were armed and Israeli fighter jets were zooming overhead. It was not long after Israel had defeated Egypt in the Sinai campaign, and the border still was tense. Our diving was limited to Israel's short stretch of coast and so was our exploration of the interior.

We drove an hour north of Eilat to King Solomon's mines, recently rediscovered through the historical memory of the Bible and the ingenuity of the archeologist Nelson Glueck. He followed Biblical descriptions that placed King Solomon's long-lost port, Ezion-geber, "beside Eilath on the shore of the Red Sea, in the land of Edom."

Near Ezion-geber, the Bible states, were King Solomon's copper mines. To locate them, Glueck took advantage of the immortality of a Bedouin place-name, Khirbet Nahas, which means "the ruin of the copper city." Long after the copper had been forgotten and the city had turned to dust, the imagery of the words lived on in the Bedouin's language. Glueck went to this place and there found piles of copper slag, pottery dating to the days of Solomon, and a great blast furnace made of natural rocks that funneled the strong prevailing wind onto burning charcoal to heat the ovens, as in the Bessemer process. Near the site of King Solomon's mines there now stands a modern copper mine from which crude copper is exported to Japan, purified, and shipped back again to Israel. Copper once more, as in the days of Solomon, has become one of the biggest businesses of Eilat.

We wandered across the desolate plain, where Solomon's slaves once tended the furnaces. We picked up potsherds, felt the searing blast of the Negev's wind, and saw the little piles of stones that were all that was left of the huts of the Edomite slaves. We came away with a piece of heavy turquoise ore that Solomon had over-looked.

In Solomon's days, when the recent domestication of the camel had opened trade routes across the desert, the chunk of ore we found would have been valuable. Copper was then worth nearly its weight in gold. It was to trade gold and jewels for copper that the Queen of Sheba went to Solomon. "She came from Arabia with a very great train of camels that bore spices and very much gold and precious stones." Then King Solomon "... gave unto the Queen of Sheba all her desire whatso-ever she asked."

The Bible tells us no more, but for centuries the kings of Ethiopia have claimed that they are descended from Solomon. As a result of the rediscovery of Solo-mon's mines, the copper of Eilat is again forging links of trade with foreign lands.

From Eilat we flew to Tel Aviv; we rented a car and drove over the barren mountains to meet the Links in Tiberias, on Galilee. The sea was six hundred feet be-low sea level, a fresh-water lake in the Jordan's descent through the Great Rift to the Dead Sea. It was here that "Jesus rebuked the winds and the sea, and there was a great calm." To come from Solomon's mines on the Red Sea to the place of Jesus' miracles was like turning a page from the Old Testament into the New.

The Sea of Galilee was always blue—not the deep blue of the Mediterranean, or the green blue of the Gulf Stream—but pastel blue. In the afternoon as the wind blew, it was flecked with white. Its Hebrew name was Lake Kinneret, because its waves made music like a harp.

When we found the Links, they and the archeologists of the expedition were as enthusiastic as if they had found a treasure of gold. The engine of the little *Reef Diver* had broken down and the crew had had to anchor to keep from being blown ashore by strong winds. One of the divers had jumped into the water to explore and had come up with a clay pot. Groping on the bottom, the Links found twenty-nine of the intact pots dating from the time of Christ. They were all together in one little area, as though a boat that was carrying them had sunk. The Links had found two stone anchors but no other trace of a boat.

In Tiberias we moved into Scottish Hospice, an outpatient clinic and a lodging place for nuns. These quiet women were faultless, so far as we could see, except for their weakness for cool, not cold, orange pop. They waged a continuous silent war with our children who liked orange pop with the same enthusiasm, but as cold as possible. The children kept turning the regulator of the icebox to cold, and the nuns as doggedly turned it back. The children and the nuns passed each other in the halls on their ways to and from the kitchen, smiled and nodded at each other, and never spoke of iceboxes.

Since the *Reef Diver's* engine was still out of commission, we had to dive from shore. We waded in from the shard-strewn beach by the ruins of the Roman baths. The water was hazy and the visibility six feet. We dived among scattered cubes of stone, the ruins of submerged buildings, and noticed bass-like fish that we recognized as "St. Peter's fish," peculiar to the Sea of Galilee, that we had eaten that day for lunch.

"Did you see that fish down there spit out that whole school of minnows?" Ann said as she popped up beside me.

I dived down to see what she was talking about, and as I approached, the cloud of tiny fishlets swam into the open mouth of one of the St. Peter's fish. The big fish retreated to a rocky cave, where it opened its mouth again and let the baby fish swim out. When I swam up to it again the performance was repeated. Perhaps it is this protection of its young that has enabled the St. Peter's fish to thrive in the face of heavy fishing from the days of the apostles to the present.

There were thousands of potsherds off the Roman Baths of Tiberias; among them George found a flint bearing the chip marks of prehistoric man. There, too, were pedestals of marble columns, for the level of the Sea of Galilee had been raised by a modern dam. We spent four days at Tiberias, exploring the bottom of the sea. In the evenings, we sat by the stormy water and looked across at the lights on the mountain tops of Syria. Then our time was nearly gone, and we had to return to Cleveland. We decided to celebrate the departure with a goat-roast feast.

Goat roasts had been a family tradition ever since we had lived in California during World War II's meat rationing and discovered that goat meat was both unrationed and good. It had become our symbol of an outdoor festival. We always barbecued them whole.

Sometimes in Cleveland, when we hadn't raised a goat of our own, it was difficult to find a farmer who had one for sale. Here, in the Middle East, we expected no trouble.

Jane and I went, confident, to the Tiberias market place looking for a live or at least a whole goat. We found plenty of goat meat—quarters, ribs, necks, liver and roasts—but no whole goat.

"But where can we get a whole goat?" Jane asked.

"The Bedouins have them," the people in the market told us; "you will have to go to the hills."

For half an hour we drove through the barren countryside looking for a Bedouin camp. When we had not been looking for them, they had seemed to be everywhere in Israel, for thousands of Bedouins roamed the desert plains as they always had, even crossing the tightly held border through friendly kibbutzim. No matter what country he roams, the Bedouin, like the gypsy, has no nationality except his own.

At last we came upon the black tent of a Bedouin, like a bat with folded wings, on the desert scrub. Beside it stood a man wearing a white kafia, blue shirt, khaki pants, and sandals. About were a few cows, a dozen goats, a flock of sheep and on a nearby hillside, a string of camels. We stopped the car before the tent, which was

about the size of the two-room houses in the kibbutz. The
Bedouin gestured for us to come in.

Inside seemed a cool oasis in the desert. The brown
goat-hair roof of the tent was as thick-woven as tweed.
Through it shone tiny glints of sunlight, like glow-
worms in a cave. The floor was covered with woven straw
mats. Around the tent was a bamboo screen four feet
high that left a couple of feet of open space between
the roof and the top of the bamboo. Through this blew a
breeze and you could look out and watch the flocks as
they grazed.

There was a brass charcoal brazier on the floor, two
engraved brass copper pots, and a beaten-up enamel
coffee pot with the enamel flaked off of the spout. Our
host pointed to himself and said, "Mohammed." We understood and, pointing to ourselves, gave our names. He
nodded. Then he reached over a bamboo barrier that
separated the living quarters from the sleeping com-
partment and picked up an armful of tan and orange
cushions which he spread in front of a low table on the
floor. He blew on the charcoal until it glowed and put a
fresh pot of coffee on the coals. He called to a child who,
with two others, was standing outside peeking over the
bamboo screen. The child ran to bring a pail of water
from the back of the tent. Mohammed washed three tiny
china coffee cups carefully, then sat down to wait for
the coffee to heat.

In the breezy shadows of the tent, we looked out at
the heat shimmering on the hills. It was as though our
senses had become dissociated from one another, our vi-

sion fixed on the glaring heat while our skin was cool and comfortable in the shade.

Conversation was impossible. The Bedouins spoke no word of English, and we knew no Arabic. We waited for the ritual of the coffee to be finished.

A thin woman with blue tattoos covering her face glanced over the bamboo, then disappeared. The coffee began to steam. I offered Mohammed a cigarette. He took it, poured the coffee, and we sat silently smoking and drinking.

When the coffee was finished, we brought up our business. We acted out the slaughter of a goat and showed Mohammed money. He knew what we wanted. We made it clear that it must be a young goat or a female goat, holding our noses to show that we didn't want a smelly buck. Mohammed nodded. We waited for his price. He indicated that he wanted twenty-five dollars. We threw up our hands.

At home we could buy a young goat sometimes for five or ten dollars. The Bedouin stayed firm. After half an hour of fruitless bargaining, knowing we had promised our children and the *Sea Diver's* crew a feast, we gave up and paid the sum and selected a young black Nubian goat.

The imperturbable Bedouin washed his hands and led the goat a hundred yards away from the tent. He slit its throat and cleaned it carefully. He wrapped the carcass in the skin and helped us pack it into the trunk of the car.

That night we built a big fire in a glade by the shore

of the lake. While we waited for the coals to be ready, we concocted a mixture of Israeli brandy, lime juice, and a native white wine. We named it Nubian Punch, and even toasted the Bedouin whose Nubian goat—at a price—had made the feast possible.

We roasted the goat whole on a grill over the charcoal, basting it from time to time with the punch and a spicy sauce with a butter base. Inside the goat was the haggis, the huge stuffing-filled stomach, sealed by tying the ends with wire. The goat was roasted slowly for two hours. When the pressure built up in the haggis, it broke open with a hiss of escaping steam. Then we chopped the meat into pieces with a cleaver and ate it in our fingers. It was brown on the outside, tender and sweet.

After the goat was gone, one of the divers played the guitar, and there was singing. Our children, even George, now were old enough to be a part of it all. The children had grown up singing ballads and old songs with us as we drove back and forth to the country and sometimes I played the ukulele and Jane, the accordion. Simple music had been a part of our life.

After the party Jane and I sat by the side of the lake. It was calmer than usual and the waves, tinkling on the rocky shore, reminded us of the sound of the little waterfall in our yard at home. At the ends of vacations, it always seemed to us that our thoughts leaped ahead and reached home before we did. Under the stars that night, the water's sound must have been the same as when the Sea of Galilee first was named Lake Kinneret.

As we sat there on the shore, talking of the children, the party, and of home, I'm sure that both of us were reminded of the threat that hung over our lives. We did not mention it.

"We've been lucky," Jane said, "to be able to see these places where so many of our traditions and beliefs were born."

I thought of the finite span of human life. Beyond a certain point it could not be prolonged. It seemed to me, on that night by Galilee, that Jane's and my interest in travel and history and archeology had added length to our lives by projection backward in time. Our experiences might not have been so rich if we had had too much concern about what the future might hold.

8

WHERE THE GODS WALKED WITH MEN— CRETE, 1961

There is a land, named Crete, fruitful and fair,
Set like a jewel in the wine-dark sea.

—Homer, *The Odyssey*

One spring evening Jane and I put a young female rabbit in the back yard. Like the old, hen-loving, buck rabbit that was already there, she had been raised without other rabbits. Nevertheless, we relied on instinct to unite the two.

The moment the buck saw the doe he dashed up to her. She fled. Round and round the yard they went until the doe, like the rape-threatened maiden in "Birth of a Nation," was cornered on the edge of the waterfall that drops into the pond. The villain slowly approached. The doe glanced over her shoulder. Then, as though she preferred death to dishonor, she plunged into the pond, bobbed up and swam to the far side.

The buck stood on the edge of the waterfall, watching as the doe climbed out of the pond, her beautiful soft-gray coat dark and dripping, and stuck flat to her ribs. Then he turned around and began to make love to a lone wood duck hen.

The buck's experience was what is called serendipity, named for the mythical Indian prince who was forever setting out to find one thing and ending up with another. That was what happened to us the time we set off to join an underwater archeological expedition off Athens and ended up on a successful one of our own off Crete.

It was in 1961, a year after our trip to Jordan and Palestine, and Jane was, insofar as could be determined, entirely well and fit for diving. I had three weeks of vacation coming. We packed our heavy diving gear, clothes, and camera equipment into canvas duffel bags and flew to Athens to meet the Links. They were with a group of Greek archeologists who were diving off the nearby island of Voulu, salvaging a first-century B.C. shipwreck, known as the "amphora wreck."

When we arrived the divers were working on a deposit of many broken and some intact amphoras lying in thirty feet of water. Pottery is the most durable of man's creations. Wood rots, metal corrodes, but a pot or its fragment remains forever. Since the ways of making pots and the style in which they are made are forever changing, archeologists can use potsherds as calendars to date ruins or wrecks. The pots that the Links were raising were huge amphora, the two-handled cargo casks of Ancient Greece and Rome. The capacity of an amphora, nine gallons, was recognized then as a standard measure. An intact amphora is valuable today for its intrinsic grace and beauty, and often for its archeological significance.

It was a tedious task to lie all day at the end of an air hose in thirty feet of water and chip carefully at pots that were incrusted in the reef. Some of the amphoras had been lying loose in the sand, and these had already been raised. Jane and I were not temperamentally fitted for the patient work that it took to separate the others from the rock. We began to read Homer, to see if he mentioned any shipwrecks that we could go in search of, and decided to visit Troy and some of the Greek islands.

Twelve hundred years before Christ was born, and two hundred years before King Solomon dug his mines, Paris, a Prince of Troy, ran off with the wife of Menelaos and started the Trojan War. Homer's accounts of this war are all we know of the history of ancient Greece. Through the pages of the *Iliad* and the *Odyssey,* as through those of the Bible, stride the geniuses and giants of those heroic times. It was to Troy, where the great war was fought, that we were heading first. We flew to Istanbul.

We had a hard time finding how to get to Troy, which is in a military zone several hundred miles from Istanbul. Our schedule was tight, because we had only a

few days of vacation left. No flights were scheduled for
any town near Troy; there was no railway; it was more
than a day's drive over bad roads. Mournful, we sat in
the bar of the hotel drinking a beer and talking about
our disappointment when the waiter, a blond-haired,
blue-eyed boy of twenty, interrupted us. "I live near
Troy."

"How do you get there?" we asked.

"By the boat to Canakkale. It leaves tomorrow
morning and you will be in by seven that night. Canakkale is only twenty-two miles from Troy. You can find a
way to get there. Then the next day the boat comes
back."

At dawn, we were at the steamship ticket office. No
one there could tell us how to get from Canakkale to
Troy, but we were sure we could find a way and be
aboard again at nine o'clock when we were told the boat
started back. In the morning, we boarded the freight-
and-passenger steamer *Alyardia,* that shuttled back and
forth three times a week between Istanbul and Canakkale. The domes and minarets of Istanbul's mosques
gleamed in the morning sun, then faded behind us as we
steamed through the Bosporus, the Sea of Marmara,
and the Dardanelles, stopping from time to time at little
towns to exchange passengers and freight. The sea was
blue and crisp, the mountains purple in the haze, and
the villages nestling beneath the mountains looked
friendly and warm. The people on the boat were good-
natured and helpful.

On shipboard, as the day wore on, we talked to

everyone we could find who spoke even a little English or French. Abdul, the ship's second officer, said we could get a taxi to carry us to Troy.

"I'll take you to the police," he said. "You must make all arrangements through them."

It was dark when we docked at Canakkale. Two-horse hackney coaches, the standard means of transportation, were lined up to meet the ship. Shoeshine boys besieged us, with elaborate black boxes, gleaming with polished brass; they leaped to their feet, inviting us, as we approached. We followed Abdul up a wide paved street, then down a narrow road to the police station. There we were given military passes, a taxi was called, and the driver was instructed to meet us at the boat at four in the morning and to have us back by sailing time.

"Now we will drink to your trip to Troy," said Abdul, and he led us up a wide, cobblestone street empty of cars. Down the street came one of the two-horse four-wheeled coaches, tall and black like the ones in which Sherlock Holmes used to dash through the streets of London, with polished brass oil lanterns at its sides and a coachman carrying a long black whip.

Abdul took us to a restaurant where, at tables spread with white cloths, the ship's crew were singing over strong raki and shish kabob. They made places for us, passed us glasses of raki, and filled our plates with the hot, broiled lamb.

We spent the night aboard ship and got up before dawn to meet the taxi for Troy. We wound through pine forest, over gorges spanned by narrow railless bridges, and up a high mountain from which we caught the glint of the distant Dardanelles. Dawn was just beginning when the road ended at a low stone building. Straight ahead was a sign that read: TROVA—TROY. We stopped and got out of the car.

To Jane and me, there was a ghostly feeling in that predawn moment when we stood hand in hand before the walls of Troy. It was as though we had been there before. We thought of the wonderful stories that had been read to us in childhood, of Hector and Achilles and Ajax, of the crafty Odysseus, of Agamemnon, Menelaos, and the gods and goddesses who descended from Olympus to intervene in the affairs of men. We had been imprinted in childhood with the tales of Troy, and it was a magic so rare that we had never expected to encounter its reality. We were suddenly transported back to the beginnings of our memories. We felt ageless, as though time stood still.

The gray, cloudy dawn made the smooth mounds of Troy's walls loom larger than they were, and made it difficult to outline the ruins of the city. Grass grew over the buried masonry, except in the excavations where trenches twenty to thirty feet deep exposed the stones.

We climbed the mound, and from its summit looked out past the ruins to the plain where the Achaeans beached their ships and Agamemnon and Achilles fought over the slave girl. There Odysseus had contrived the wooden horse, and there Hector's naked body was dragged.

We walked down to the field where there was a

shepherd boy, his flock bleating softly in the dawn. The earth was covered with potsherds and the rubble of Troy. The boy showed us a handful of coins that he had found in the field as he grazed his flocks. We bought a few, then returned to the ruins, their mounded battlements best seen from below, towering seventy feet above the plain.

There was time that morning for only an impression of Troy and its nine cities that have been uncovered, one on top of another. The first city was built in 3000 B.C.; the second, where a treasure at first thought to be King Priam's had been found, was a much older civilization than King Priam's Troy. Six cities rose and fell at the site before the Troy described by Homer was built.

Schliemann, the father of modern archeology, had come here, and with obsessional faith in Homer's descriptions, followed them and discovered "King Priam's treasure." Later, at Mycenae, again following Homer's descriptions, he found the grave circle of the kings, the golden "death mask of Agamemnon" and the jewels of the Mycenaean court.

Homer's epic poems are the Bible of Greece. They tell of gods and kings and men who lived at the same time as the heroes of our Old Testament. Like the Old Testament, the historical memories of the *Iliad* and the *Odyssey* repeatedly have proved to be accurate.

The sun was rising and gave color to a flower, growing scarlet from a crack between two immense blocks of brown stone. It was as though the blood of the Trojans still flowed on the walls of Troy. The wind, so often mentioned by Homer in his descriptions, had started to blow and bent the flower with its force. In the gray light of the gusty dawn we sensed the spirit of Homer in the grassy mounds. The wind, now blowing hard, brought to mind a passage in the *Odyssey* about a storm that had wrecked Menelaos' ships on their return from Troy. Nestor was telling Telemachos what happened to Menelaos on his way home to Sparta.

"Let's get out the *Odyssey*," Jane said, and we reread the account:

> *Zeus Almighty decreed a hard road for them to travel: he poured out a hurricane of whistling winds and monstrous swollen waves mountain-high. Then he cut the fleet in two, and brought part of them to Crete, where the Cydonians are settled about the stream of Iardanos. There is a smooth cliff running down steep into the sea at the verge of Gortyn, over the misty deep, where the wind from the south-west drives a great wave against the western headland toward Phaistos, and a little bit of stone keeps off the great wave. So far they came, and the men escaped death with great trouble; but the ships were all smashed to pieces on those rocks by the sea.*

Our minds were set afire. We decided to follow the book as Schliemann had done, and see if we could find the remains of Menelaos' ships. Serendipity was beginning to work.

We returned to Istanbul and the next day set off by plane for the "land, named Crete, fruitful and fair, set like a jewel in the wine-dark sea." We had no diving equipment other than face plates and flippers. We had our book and continued to read: "There are many men beyond number and ninety cities: There are Cydonians, illustrious Pelagians, and Dorians of the waving hair." Here, Homer continued, King Minos was in command of the sea, the same mighty Minos who sacrificed Athenian youths and maidens to the man-eating minotaur kept in the labyrinth, and whose fleets sailed to distant ports for ivory, gold, and slaves.

Through the ages, time's dark mystery had settled over Crete. The Minoan civilization flourished in 2000 B.C. at the time of the Middle Kingdom of Egypt, but it lived only in legend by the time of Homer who sang of "a dancing place, bright gleaming" at Knossos. Homer's descriptions of Crete were thought to be fanciful until the British archeologist, Sir Arthur Evans, unearthed the Palace of King Minos and the remains of that splendid civilization. Evans spent his life excavating the palace at Knossos, a city in itself, that once housed over a thousand people. These findings and tablets, inscribed in one of man's earliest written languages, proved again that Homer's descriptions were accurate, even in detail.

When we landed in Crete, we rented a car at Heraklion, once the port of Knossos. We knew where to go from Homer's description: it was on the ten-mile niche of the southern coast, where the little harbor of Matela lay.

"But no one lives there," the travel agent told us. "You will have no place to stay."

We decided to take our chances and hurried off. Our vacation time was nearly spent, there were only two days left. Two of Homer's landmarks, Gortyn and Phaistos, were on the way to Matela.

We drove over winding roads, chiseled out of mountainsides with no banking or railing. Buses and cars were gradually replaced by mule carts and donkeys. This was central Crete, desert plains and bare hills with vineyards and olive trees on their lower slopes. There were dusty white villages of stucco and stone, the children shouting and waving at us, the girls carrying water on their heads in graceful amphora. And always there were black-dressed women sitting in their doorways as if in perpetual mourning perhaps for the passing of the Minoan culture, when barebreasted women rode and hunted with their husbands and were gay and dominant features of the life of Crete.

Near the village of Mires was the partially excavated site of Homer's Gortyn, once the capital of a mighty kingdom that included Lybia and extended to the sea. Over its rich Minoan remains were built Greek, Roman, and Byzantine cities, each in turn fallen into rubble and dust.

From the hills of Gortyn, the road descended to the plains of Messara. Excavated clay tablets have listed inventories of arms and goods, and the names of more than nineteen thousand people who once owned herds of sheep there; now it was a parched plain dotted with olive trees. With irrigation it could be made to yield the fruits and grains that once supported the mighty city of Phaistos, and enabled its Minoan king to build a palace even larger than the one at Knossos.

From Phaistos on there were no more cars on the road, only donkeys and an occasional horse ridden by a peasant in high black Turkish boots. The wind blew up so strong from the Lybian Sea that great branches were blown from the olive trees, and the people were busy gathering them for fuel. We passed Mount Ida, where legend says Zeus in his infancy was fed by the sacred bees and the goat Amaltheia, then we climbed a range of coastal hills and started down a gentle valley. We found the hitherto dirt road was paved with big cobblestones like a Roman road, and on the right there was a crumbling stone wall. We stopped to examine it; some of the stones were fragments of marble columns.

As we drove on over the cobblestoned road, rounding the side of a hill, we were totally unprepared for the sight that lay ahead. On the Bay of Matela a strong wind, like the one Homer described, was blowing from the west, and the breaking waves poured up on the sand of a crescent beach. On each side of the beach were tall cliffs of wind-smoothed rock that clasped the bay securely and guarded it against all but a due west wind. The rock of those cliffs was honeycombed with caves.

We stopped the car and got out to gaze at the panorama of sea, cliffs and caves. The caves seemed deserted; but then we heard a shout. In a moment the mouths of the caves were filled with people. An old man waved a welcome and came toward us. He had great white mustachios and was wearing black baggy Turkish pants. It is said that the next Mohammedan prophet was to be born not of woman but of man, and there must be room in his pants for the carrying of the baby prophet. The man spoke to us in Greek, and we shrugged and smiled.

Out of a primitive church cave, part of a catacomb cut in solid stone and blocked by the rubble of centuries, came a priest in purple robe, with a flowing white beard. He greeted us in the Greek tongue and led us to his cave chapel. Inside was an icon of the Virgin, a silver-faced portrait of a saint, and a smoky old canvas painting that the priest pointed to. "Byzantine," he said, raising fingers to indicate that it dated from the seventeenth century. He showed us the bell of the church, a fragment of a German bomb, left from the German occupation of Crete in World War II.

A crowd of boys gathered and followed us as we walked along a road cut in the cliff to the biggest cave. It was wide mouthed and shallow, nestled under the overhang of the cliff. In its shadows a dozen windbound fishermen were sipping little cups of coffee and tall, thin glasses of water. Deeper in the cave on the right was a bar. Straight ahead a small door led into a second cave, carved out of the cool limestone rock where a great barrel of wine was stored.

As we approached, the men stood up and with smiles and bows offered us chairs and a table.

"*Germanicos?*" one of them asked.

"*Americanos,*" I replied.

The man behind the bar turned and spoke rapidly in Greek to one of the fishermen, who left the cave. He returned shortly, accompanied by a wiry old man with a white moustache and dark glasses.

"Where you from?" he said.

"Cleveland," Jane told him.

"That was my home for forty years," he said. "You know Lorain?"

Lorain, thirty miles from Cleveland; we knew it well.

"I built ships in Lorain. I am Stanislas Merikavis, and I welcome you to Matela."

Stanislas said something to the man behind the bar, and we too were served tiny cups of thick sweet coffee spiced with herbs and given tall glasses of water to sip. We asked Stanislas about the caves and the people living in them.

"The caves are Greco-Roman tombs," Stanislas said, "and the people are farmers who come here in summer to bathe and escape the heat. Why do you come to Matela?"

Jane showed him the *Odyssey* and pointed out the marked passage. "We have come here to find these shipwrecks."

"Then you must talk to the schoolteacher." Stanislas beckoned to a powerfully built man, whom he introduced as Elias Fassoulakis. He was so dintinguished-looking that we called him "Professor" at once. He could not speak English, but we communicated with gestures and an *interlingua* of classical roots.

The Professor knew Homer, much of it by heart. We showed him our copy of the *Odyssey,* and he at once began to recite in Greek a long passage. His voice was deep and musical, and he beat his fist, and the fishermen smiled and rocked to the rhythm of the ancient poem. As we heard the Professor recite, we understood why Homer's descriptions were so accurate. The ballads of the Trojan War had been frozen in unchangeable meter and rhyme.

Stanislas told the Professor what we were looking for and then slowly translated the passage. As the Professor listened, he became excited. He pointed to the mountains behind the sandy beach, "Phaistos, Gortyn, Iardanos," he cried and turned to the fishermen, speaking to them in Greek. When Stanislas came to "the smooth cliff running down steep into the sea," the fishermen nodded their heads and one of them gestured to the northwest. Then came the "little bit of stone that keeps off the great wave," and there was animated discussion.

"The teacher says it's by Papadoplaka, the Sacred Rock," our translator told us. "You have found the right man. He knows the place you mean."

The high winds were still blowing. The sea was too rough to go to the Sacred Rock by boat, but the Professor offered to show us the caves and the sunken harbor of Matela. We accepted and walked with him to the end of the bay.

The beach was made of bits of ancient pottery, polished pebbles, and marble of many colors. The waves

rolled in on them and we thought of Matthew Arnold's
"Dover Beach":

> *Listen! you hear the grating roar*
> *of pebbles which the waves draw back, and fling,*
> *At their return, up the high strand . . .*
> *Sophocles long ago*
> *Heard it on the Aegean, and it brought*
> *Into his mind the turbid ebb and flow*
> *Of human misery . . .*

As we looked across the bay, we saw the outline of
buildings under the water and how some of the lower
tombs now were partly sunk beneath the sea. The Professor led us across the beach, up the cliff on the north
side of the bay, and into one of the tombs. We barely fitted through the doorway. Inside there was a little fire of
twigs and over it hung a black pot. Back in the shadows
sat two children, and a peasant woman, black-dressed,
got up out of a niche in the far wall where she had been
lying on a mat.

"*Os*," the Professor said, tapping his shin bone and
then pointing to the niche the woman had left. We understood that bones had once rested there.

The Professor showed us more tombs, most of them
inhabited by the vacationing peasants. Some were
roomy and had four or five burial niches with smaller
niches for lamps, ornaments, or offerings. Water was
lapping into the doorways of the lower tombs and in
some only the tops of the doors were above the water.
Perhaps there were others, completely submerged. Beneath the Greco-Roman ruins might be sunk the re-

mains of older civilizations. We decided to look under the water, even though the waves were still beating high.

We went back to the car to get our face plates and flippers, and then swam out along the cliff, the waves sloshing over our faces. The water was cloudy, but we could see enough to recognize an underwater tomb. I dove first through the submerged doorway and into a cave which was square-hewn, with a thick wall in its center. There were niches in the walls like the caves above, but this tomb had holes two feet square carved in the floor. When I came up into the gloomy air space, the surf surged hollowly against the rock.

Jane joined me in the air space and then we dived. Lying on the dark stone floor, chalk white in the blue water-filtered light, was a heap of bones. It was a macabre setting in the somber shadows of the cave—the skeleton gleaming below, and the slosh of the water echoing in the niches.

As we swam out of the sunken tomb and along the cliff looking down at the smooth rock bottom we came upon a deep rectangular hole cut in the solid rock bottom. It was in water twelve feet deep and the pit went down ten feet further in the solid stone.

"It looks like a shaft tomb," Jane told me.

We had seen the pre-Phoenician shaft tombs of Biblos, on the coast of Lebanon, some of them sixty feet deep. The stone pit below us was filled with rubble just as those at Biblos had been, where funeral treasures of gold and jewels had been found.

We dived down to examine the shafts further and

there, caught between the rocks, was a round metal object twelve inches in diameter. We came up breathless. "It's the black color of silver salts. It's a silver plate!" I was sure.

The plate had what looked like a candle holder in the middle of it. It was firmly wedged between two great rocks. As we took turns diving down and trying to work it loose, a group of children came to watch us from the cliffs. Finally we pried the plate loose and brought it up. The children cheered; then one of them said something, and the cheers changed to cries of warning. The children edged away from the cliff, shaking their heads.

Suddenly, like Triton emerging from the deep, a man carrying a three-tined fish spear and wearing a face plate surfaced beside us. "You'd better drop that," he said in English. "It's part of a land mine. Four years ago one of them killed four children."

We dropped the mine and thanked him. He introduced himself, Nicholas Cougerakis, the tax collector of the village of Mires. We asked him if he had ever seen any signs of shipwrecks on the bottom by the Sacred Rock.

"I have seen strange things on the bottom around Papadoplaka," he told us. "They look like piles of broken pottery, but I was spearfishing and didn't pay attention."

In the Mediterranean, most ancient shipwrecks are marked by the amphora in which the Greeks carried cargoes of wine, grain, and oil. It seemed to be a very old shipwreck that our friend was describing.

"I'll take you there, if you're not afraid of high places and rough water," Nicholas said. "A goatherd once showed me a way down the cliff."

We invited the Professor to come too, and with Nicholas as our guide and interpreter, drove back down the coast. When we came to the Roman cobblestoned road, Nicholas motioned us to stop, and we set out on foot across a wide flat plateau between the mountains. The Professor pointed to a spot on the hill at the right side of the plain, where deep grooves were cut in the shelving rock to direct water into a reservoir.

"Cisterna neolithica," he said, and *"nero,"* which is the Greek word for water.

Everywhere were broken tiles and potsherds. The plain on which we were walking was strewn with rubble of a Greco-Roman city that the Professor called Bouboulia. Nowhere was there a trace of an archeologist's dig. As we walked seaward across the shard-strewn plain, we heard the tinkle of bells in the hills, and a goatherd waved to us from his flock. Ahead the plain was deserted, an untended grave of forgotten civilizations. We walked on, the salt wind in our faces. Then we came to a precipice, four hundred feet high. Ahead lay the Lybian Sea described by Homer, not blue like most seas but a dark purple, flecked with white. To the right of the cliff, the land was cut away in a shallow bay where breakers rolled up on a smooth expanse of bright white sand. We stood on the edge, against the wind.

The air over the sea was misty, just as Homer had described it. Beyond the bay towered a range of mountains that trapped the moisture in a pocket of stone. "It is always misty on this part of the coast," Nicholas told us over the wind.

The Professor pointed seaward to an invisible island. "Ogygia," he shouted. "Calypso."

It was on the island of Ogygia that "the beautiful and terrible Calypso" held Odysseus captive for seven long years. She promised him perpetual youth if he would stay with her forever.

"Phaistos," the Professor said, pointing northeast, and *"Gortyn."* His voice was loud and insistent. It was towards Phaistos, Homer said, that the southwest wind drove the great wave.

"Iardanos," the Professor shouted and pointed a mile due north to a spot where a dry river bed met the sea. Was this the "stream of Iardanos" of which Homer wrote?

"Papadoplaka," the Professor persisted in an almost Homeric meter, and he pointed to a great black rock, the Sacred Rock, that stood two hundred yards from shore. Here surely was Homer's "little bit of stone that kept off the great wave from the southwest." The only thing that was missing in this topographic reincarnation of Homer's tales was the "smooth cliff running down steep into the sea."

The Professor motioned us back, as we crept out to look over the edge. We were on an overhang, and on the beach below was a jumble of rock falls that had carried with them the ruins of the ancient city. Nicholas disappeared over the edge of the precipice at a spot marked by a gnarled juniper stump that lined up with the

Sacred Rock and the distant island of Ogygia. He
started down a goat trail beneath the overhanging rock.
The descent was precipitous; we scrambled over rock
falls and slipping land slides. Bayonet bushes scratched
our legs; our feet, fumbling for footholds, crushed pungent wild mint and thyme. Our thighs grew weak and
our legs trembled. The sea rumbled ominously on the
rocks below. Our guide was surefooted and imperturbable. The Professor, slipping and sliding as badly as we,
brought up the rear.

In the cliff, a hundred feet above the sea, there was a
yard-wide stratum of fossilized oyster shells. Below, in
the late afternoon sun, a deep red glow was cast. There
were great chunks of the ancient city, fallen down the
precipice onto the beach, leaving slides of red earth filled
with the debris of former civilizations. The land slide
was studded with the fragments of things once used for
everyday living, pieces of pottery, building tiles, and
handles of amphora.

In the rubble of this city that the Professor had
called Bouboulia, we found a tapered, rectangular, pottery artifact, three inches high, with a little hole drilled
in one side of its narrow end. We had never seen a Greco-
Roman artifact like this and neither had the Professor.
We took it with us, for we thought it might be Minoan,
used, perhaps, by the Cydonians who, Homer told us,
were settled here near the Iardanos River. Bouboulia
might once have been one of the ninety Cretan cities of
which Homer wrote, we suggested to the Professor, and
he agreed.

The beach was made of huge broken rocks. We

climbed around them along the cliff and after wading around a point of rock, came to a cove where the waves were splashing up on red dirt and washing it slowly into the sea. On the beach was an oval stone three feet long with a round hole near one end that looked as if it had been drilled there. Five yards away was another one with a hole. They looked just like the stone anchors that the Links had found in the Sea of Galilee.

"Out there by Papadoplaka is where the pottery is," Nicholas said and he put on his face plate. We put on ours and our flippers.

The water was rough, shoulder-high waves breaking on the rocky beach. We waded into the surf and then dove through one of the breakers. As we swam down into the cold still water below, it was as though we had plunged from the turmoil of the moment into the long-dead era of Menelaos and the Trojan War.

The water was turbid from the storm, and visibility only six feet. All we could see on the bottom were ominous shadows and eelgrass swaying across smooth bedrock. Groping along the ocean floor twenty-five feet deep and one hundred yards from shore, we found scattered pieces of red pottery. We couldn't tell whether they had been washed out from the city, or were part of a wreck. Nicholas could not find the pile of pottery he was looking for. We were tired from fighting the rough waves; there was nothing to do until the weather became better. We said goodbye to Nicholas, who had to return to his village.

Back at Matela we had supper in a bar-restaurant

cave. Facing us in the twilight was the cliff, with lamps
and little fires glowing in the caves. Seaward, between
headlands that might have been the pillars of Hercules,
lay the deep blue of the Mediterranean and the misty
shores of Calypso's enchanted island. We sipped our
oozos on the balcony and reread the story of Calypso and
Odysseus.

When Zeus' messenger arrived at Calypso's great
cave, he found her, Homer says, ". . . with her beautiful
hair flowing over her shoulders. A great fire blazed on
the hearth, and the burning logs of cedar and juniper
wafted their fragrant scent far over the island. Calypso
sat within by her loom, singing in a lovely voice, and
shooting her golden shuttle to and fro. A thick coppice
of trees grew round the cave, alder and aspen and sweet-
smelling cypress. There the birds would sail to rest on
their outspread wings, owls and falcons and long-
tongued sea-ravens who busy themselves about the waters. Over the gaping mouth of the cave trailed a luxurious grape vine, with clusters of ripe fruit; and four rills
of clear water ran in a row close together, winding over
the ground. Beyond were soft meadows thick with vio-
lets and wild celery. That was a sight to gladden the
very gods."

Time, we decided, had wrought little change in the
tastes of man. It would be hard to imagine a more idyllic
spot to while away the years. Nor, in those ancient
days, were the ways of a man with a nymph too different
from what, under similar circumstances, they might be
today, for Odysseus, after spending the day ". . . sitting

upon the rocks or the sands staring at the barren sea and sorrowing" for his wife Penelope, was wont, when the sun went down and darkness came, to return to Calypso and then, Homer says, "... these two lay down in the corner of the lofty cave, and enjoyed their love together." As we read, and tasted the *oozo,* it seemed that we could hear the distant singing of the nymph across the misty sea.

The restaurateur, Radamanthus, whom we had met that afternoon, had killed a chicken, and brought out tomatoes, bread, and goat cheese. Then he tapped his keg of retzina. In ancient times wine was stored in amphora, and to prevent evaporation and leakage through the porous clay, the jugs were coated with resin which gave a flavor to the wine that has become an acquired taste and lives on today in the Greeks' love of their retzina wine.

After supper we decided that Greek hospitality hadn't changed since the days when Odysseus, disguised as a beggar, stopped at his swineherd's shack and was given "bread and wine to fill the belly and a heap of sheepskins to lie on." The Professor found blankets for us. We curled up in a "sea-hollowed cave" and, like Odysseus, slept a long, enchanted sleep.

We were up with the sun and found a flat calm on the sea. After breakfast of bread, cheese, eggs fried and soaked in olive oil, and Turkish coffee, we borrowed a pickaxe and jumped into Radamanthus' fishing boat. Somber as his namesake, the uncorruptible judge of Phaistos, he stood in the middle of his boat facing forward as he rowed us out of the harbor.

The air was just as Homer described it. It was not fog, the air close by seemed clear, yet Calypso's island was lost in the mist and the tops of the mountains were unreal. Then we saw the missing piece of the puzzle. Sloping down from the top of the mountain was a smooth, unbroken expanse of naked rock, the "smooth cliff running down steep into the sea at the verge of Gortyn." Now all the landmarks checked with Homer.

When we were opposite the Sacred Rock, we pointed out to Radamanthus where we wanted to go. He anchored and we put on our face plates and flippers and jumped in. The water had cleared overnight.

Below us was a smooth rock bottom and running shoreward from the Sacred Rock was a reef of huge, broken rocks. Meeting this natural reef at right angles was an unusual formation, fifty feet long, ten feet wide, and waist high. It was white on its top, like a recently broken coral reef, but it was made of round, waterworn stones, different from the limestone rocks of the reef.

"There's something queer about that reef," I called to Jane.

"It's wreckage," she said. "Those stones look like ballast."

We dived down to examine them and found they were ballast stones, and among them were pieces of amphora—piles of bottoms, tops, handles and fragments of their broken bellies. Here, exactly at the spot Homer described, was an ancient shipwreck.

One hundred feet away was a second pile of wreckage, this one still in the shape of a ship. It was waist high and made up mainly of broken amphora. Shoreward was a reef of round stones and pottery, as though several ships had been churned together against the rocks.

We dived down to try to salvage some of the artifacts. With no air supply it was a struggle to stay down twenty-five feet where the wreckage lay. The pottery was stuck so fast to the bottom by the sediment of centuries that we had to use the pickaxe to break our samples. Slowly we drifted upward with each artifact. As we surfaced, we realized we were breaking again the barrier of time. But there was a plane to catch that afternoon. We packed the artifacts in the car and drove back to Heraklion.

In the Candia Archeological Museum, Professor Nicholas Platon, the director, was cordial and interested. "This is a Minoan loom weight," he said of the little tapered relic that we had found on the land slide at Bouboulia. "It is the first Minoan artifact I have seen from that area." Then he questioned us about the underwater caves and the shaft tomb that we had explored in the Bay of Matela.

"Archeologists have not yet explored that area underwater," he said. "It's something that should be done as soon as possible."

We got out our well-used Homer and showed him the passage that had guided us and the fragments of amphora that we had raised. We told him that it seemed there were three separate shipwrecks on that reef.

Professor Platon looked carefully at the amphora handles and necks. "Greco-Roman," he said finally. "Second century B.C." Platon was an expert on pottery and could date a find to within a century. Although the amphora fragments were not from Menelaos' wrecks, nevertheless we consoled ourselves. The samples had come from only one of the three wrecks. Our spot might be one of those windblown pockets, well-known to mariners, into which, through the centuries, countless ships have been blown. Off Turkey, on a reef only a few hundred yards long, divers have found fifteen ancient shipwrecks, each of a different era. Menelaos' ships, we thought, might lie side by side with the second-century wreck whose pottery Professor Platon had dated.

Jane and I, with the help of Homer and serendipity, had found the three wrecks in only an hour of diving and with the use of only face plates and flippers. What else might lie between the western headland and the Sacred Rock we had no way of knowing. The topography of the area checked exactly with Homer's description of the place where Menelaos' five "dark-prowed" ships were wrecked. They had been laden, Homer said, with "captive women dressed in their best and with goblets and tripods and cauldrons of gold." In time underwater archeologists may uncover the gold by moving the heaps of amphora and ballast stones that mark the wrecks.

Jane and I wanted to be there when they did. As we left Heraklion we promised ourselves that we would return with plans and equipment to explore again this history-haunted coast. When we made our pledge we had no way of knowing that the time allotted to us was to be so short.

9

THE WHISPERING
OF THE DREAM—
BANGKOK, 1962

*If you could hear the whispering of the
dream you would hear no other sound.*

—Kahlil Gibran, *The Prophet*

Three months after our return from Crete,
Jane and I were in a marsh south of Cleveland, walking
together through the autumn twilight and listening to
the whistle of wings as the ducks pitched in through the
sunset. Jane rubbed her neck.

"That darn gun must have kicked me," she said.
"My shoulder's stiff."

Jane had not been shooting much that day. Moreover, earlier in the week she'd had an unexplained fever.
Both of us, I think, were wondering if these were connected with the trouble of nearly four years ago.

The next day Jane's chest was X-rayed. There were two little round discs in the lung fields. In addition there was an enlargement of the lymph nodes to the right of the center of the chest. All of this was on the opposite side from the original tumor. It represented a spread of the cancer through the blood.

Jane and I reviewed the X rays with the radiologists. They thought that the two blood-borne tumors in the lung had in turn spread back to the lymph nodes that drained that section of the lung. Surgeons agreed that the tumors should be removed. Although there was little hope for permanent cure, there was good chance of controlling the symptoms caused by the tumors in the chest.

On the evening before the operations we were sitting in the glassed-in porch that overlooks the back yard. We were sipping drinks and talking about the wood ducks we had raised that summer. For two years we had been trying to establish a colony of free-winged wood ducks that would fly in and out of our pond at will and return to our yard to nest. When autumn came the young ones always grew restless and flew away.

There was a flash of wings against the sunset. Four ducks encircled the yard, flew out of sight behind the house, returned, and with wings set teetered in under the telephone wires and pitched fluttering into the pond. This was what we had been waiting for, our colony returned. The wood ducks were the ones we had raised that summer. They went directly to the food dish, making their soft whistles to one another.

"It's an omen," Jane said, entranced. "Everything's going to be all right tomorrow."

Next morning, on our way to the operating room, she stopped in at the hospital cafeteria and bought some doughnuts. "This is Monday," she said, "our day in the lab. I want to leave these for everyone for the coffee break."

The operation went well. But I could not keep my mind on my work that day. The problems that my patients and their families had were too close to my own. When I returned home that night I found on my pillow a note: "I will return."

Jane came home on the second day after the operation. Three days later was the traditional Clinic Christmas Dance before which, every year, we gave a dinner for the staff and residents of the surgical department. Jane presided as usual. Three weeks later, after the radiation of the nodes at the center of the chest was completed, we flew to Nassau with Susie and George. Both the older girls were then married. We joined Jane's sister and her family in a sailing cruise of the Bahamas. Their two boys were the same ages as Susie and George, and the two families were very close, each often leaving children with the other when they departed or taking them along with their own on vacations. Before the trip was over Jane was paddling around with face plate and flippers, taking pictures of the reefs.

Illness, it seems, is often what the patient makes of it. Its duration can be prolonged or considerably contracted. To her illness, Jane reacted with simplicity. She was aware that there was little chance of permanently curing a cancer that had spread to the lungs. Yet she showed no trace of fear. There was sorrow but not dread. To Jane, faith in those she loved was infinite, "heaven was here and now." The only emotion she expressed was an occasional word of regret that her share of time might be so short. There was no negative quality in Jane's character; she was directed to action and accomplishment. Her philosophy was expressed in a note to our second daughter, Joan, written at the time of her operation. "Take a good look into the heart of the universe, Joan. Somewhere out there you will find that time and space are infinite and beyond our comprehension. That leaves us the alternative of living from day to day."

After her convalescence Jane wanted to go back to Crete again to meet Nicholas and the Professor and continue the search for Menelaos' "dark-prowed" ships.

Since Jane had never been to Japan and neither of us had seen the Far East, we decided to fly west to Crete, stopping on the way in Japan, Hong Kong, Thailand, Indo-China and India. Of all these places, Thailand was the most important, for there we had a friend we loved, Dr. Sem Pring-Puang-Gen, of Bangkok, a philosopher as well as a leading surgeon of Siam.

I had met Sem thirteen years before in my operating room in Cleveland, where I had noticed him intently watching and making notes. He had been sent to the United States by the Thailand government to study American surgery. He was then my age, forty-one. His expression seemed placid as a Buddha's, but his behavior was the opposite. I had liked him at once and invited him home to dinner that night. There were oysters. He asked Jane for an apron, and helped us open them. He worked dexterously, with a special Thai twist.

As we were eating, Sem began to tell us about the north of Siam, up near the Burmese border, where he was born. "There are great teakwood forests there. The elephants pull out the logs. Someday you must visit me and we will go together to see them. Elephants understand just what they must do, and they think almost like a man. That is why they do it so well. And there are tigers up there too. They come down to the villages at night and kill cattle and men."

"We've got bears in the country here," I told Sem.

"Bears?" He was sober.

"Certainly." I became enthusiastic, forgetting it was midwinter and any bears that might be around would be sound asleep. "We'll go bear hunting tomorrow!"

Twenty-five miles east of Cleveland, we had a weekend cabin. There was no electricity, no telephone, no heat. In the surrounding woods and rocky places were foxes and grouse and deer that still roamed the area. In recent years even a timber wolf was killed there, and on several occasions reliable observers reported seeing a bear.

In the morning we set out, heavily armed with Saur-Mauser rifles. For two hours we walked through the deep snow, following the tracks of animals, including those of a neighbor's St. Bernard dog whose footprints were about as big as a bear's. Jane and I were so eloquent with our guest that we almost talked ourselves into expecting a bear to appear, too.

Finally, chilled and with our rifles still unfired, we returned to the cabin. We built a big apple-wood fire, heated buttered rum, poured it in mugs, then plunged a red-hot poker in to mull it. Evening settled over the woods outside, our fire burned low, and as we lay back on the big bearskin hearth rug, the rum made us warm and expansive.

Sem, with quiet intensity, began to tell Jane and me of the Buddhist faith. Like Christianity, it must mean different things to different people, but to Sem it was a way of life of infinite adaptability. It was a positive philosophy that found a time and place for all things good. That night, before the fire, Jane and I promised Sem that one day we would visit his far-off land.

Now, thirteen years later, we were arriving in Bangkok, on the way to Crete. Sem was at the airport to greet us. In Bangkok, everything was a mixture of East and West in a stage of transition. There were saffron-robed, shaven-headed priests everywhere on the wide, traffic-filled streets. Golden, pagoda-roofed Buddhist temples, of which there were over three hundred in the city, stood beside modern buildings.

The next morning, the three of us boarded a DC-3 and flew for three hours over the seemingly endless rice paddies of the Chao Phraya Valley. Then we were over wooded hills, with the mountains of Burma on the left, and soon we were landing at Chiang Mai, where Sem was born. It was the capital of the Northern Province and the second largest city of Thailand.

We were eager to see the elephants that Sem described to us so long ago. The teak forests, where they worked, were a four-hour drive north from Chiang Mai, over winding mountainous roads, past streams, farms, villages, and forests until finally there were no more clearings, only mountains and trees. We parked the car in a forest and set out on foot down a broad, wooded path. There was elephant spoor on the trail, tracks and dung.

There were three elephants working in that Thai lumber camp. The first we saw was walking down a stream bed dragging a teak log, and sitting on his head was a wizened little man. This was its oozie, Sem explained, a man who'd grown up from boyhood in charge of that particular elephant. The elephant we watched was called Posom. The others were Doik and Duang, and they too, with their oozies on their backs, were pulling the logs out of the forest and stacking them in piles. They seemed to have an innate sense of symmetry, as they raised the logs on their tusks, stacked them, and pushed them about with their trunks until the piles were neat and orderly. This part of the work they did of their own accord, without commands from their oozies. As they worked with the great logs the elephants and their riders blended perfectly with the forest.

"They look as if they had always been here," Jane said.

"They have," Sem said. "Throughout Thai history we have used them for work and war. Our elephants are treated as if almost human. Once, when the mother of a sacred white elephant in the palace of Mandalay died, twenty young Burmese women were used as wet nurses for the baby elephant."

Sem told us that in many ways people and elephants were alike. If you allowed for the differences in maturity at birth, the life cycles of elephants and men were parallel. The elephant carried its baby for twenty-one months and when the calf was born, all covered with hair, it weighed about two hundred pounds. A few minutes after birth it could walk and get around, just the way a one-year-old baby did, for both the human at one year and the elephant at birth were the same age, twenty-one months after conception. Sem said that both human and elephant babies began to eat without help at the same relative time—the elephants at three months after birth and humans at fifteen. At the age of thirteen years the elephant reached sexual maturity, and at twenty was fully grown.

For hours we watched the elephants working. Sem said that at sixty-five years they would be retired from work and let loose in the jungle, where some of them might live to be one hundred. The oozies told us, with Sem interpreting, that if the elephant didn't get an annual vacation he went on strike. Five days a week and eight hours a day, they claimed, was as much work as an elephant could be persuaded or forced to do. Perhaps it was not the elephant who set this work schedule. The oozie spoke for the elephant and the two acted as one.

From the jungle we drove back to Chiang Mai. "Would you like to see an oriental drug store?" Sem asked.

He took us into a shop filled with dried herbs, bright-colored elixirs, and exotic powders, including powdered rhinoceros horn, a favorite remedy for impotence. Years before, in London, on St. Catherine's docks, in a space that seemed a quarter of a mile long, we had seen great stacks of elephant tusks, and there were also heaps of rhinoceros horns and the single horns of narwhals, five feet long, sharp at the tips and threaded like screws. The narwhal horn was sold to the Orient as unicorn horn, which, like the horn of the rhinoceros, was considered a phallic symbol of potency. The rhinoceros horns were imported from Africa, then stamped in London "to prove them genuine," and next reexported to the Orient, where they ended up as a powder in drug stores like the one in Chiang Mai.

"At least it's harmless," Sem said, "and probably it is about as effective as most remedies for that condition."

We flew back to Bangkok the next day. There Sem took us through the Woman's Hospital, which, under his direction, had grown from seventy-five to fourteen hundred beds, and was still growing. It was made up of a series of two-story pavilions connected by outdoor covered walks. The modern equipment included a laboratory for putting catheters into diseased hearts, an image amplifier for making motion pictures of the circulation of injected dye, and a laboratory for the early diagnosis of cancer by "Pap smears."

The most spectacular department, we thought, was the obstetrical one. There in 1961, nearly fourteen thousand babies were delivered; forty babies a day, one every half hour. Sem took us to the delivery area where there was an assembly line of baby-filled bassinets. When a new baby was added to one end of the line, an older one was taken off the other and given to its mother. There were fifteen to twenty women lying in a large ward, in labor.

"What do you give them for the pain?" we asked Sem, for the women were not making a sound.

"No narcotics," Sem said, "sometimes a mild sedative, that is all."

Western women, Sem told us, were more apprehensive about delivery than the Orientals. He had delivered a number of women connected with Western embassies, and found that they usually required more sedation and anesthesia than the Thais. We discussed the nature of pain. Sem thought that basically it was like an emotion.

I agreed with him, and spoke of the imprintation of terror that the needle had made on the children of today. Thirty years ago, before children were subjected to frequent needle punctures for immunizations, it was quite simple to perform operations under local anesthesia and have the patient complain of little or no pain. The sensitivity of tissue to the pain of cutting or clamping is confined largely to the skin; the deeper tissues are sensitive mainly to stretching and pulling. If the skin was anesthetized, if the patient had confidence in the surgeon, and if the operation was conducted gently, it was not considered painful. That was before people became conditioned against needles. Today screaming children are restrained by their mothers while the doctor injects the necessary vaccines. When the children grow up they may faint at the sight of a needle, or be so terrified that they lose self-control and interpret each sensation of pressure as an unbearable pain.

Sem had a pair of Siamese twins in the hospital, waiting operation, and he took us to see them. They were nine months old and were sitting up in bed, crying, and apparently fighting with each other. They usually seemed happy, the nurse told us. It is in the nature of living things to be content with the life to which they are born, at least until they become aware of some other.

Siamese twins, connected through the tissues of the upper abdomen, occurred once in every thirty-four thousand births at the Woman's Hospital, the same incidence as elsewhere where records are kept. Doctor Sem was the world's greatest authority on the operation to separate them. He had operated successfully on five pairs with the loss of only one of the ten babies. While we were in Bangkok, he had a call from a surgeon in California who had Siamese twins as patients and was asking for advice.

When we left Woman's Hospital and were on the way to Sem's home, he said, "In the morning we will go through the klongs first."

Early the next day the three of us were in a boat
putting down the river and through the klongs of Bangkok. They were a system of canals more extensive than
those of Venice, and had survived from ancient times.
The water was filled with every conceivable kind of
craft: rafts of floating logs, dories pushed by sculling
oars, motor launches like ours, and outboards, whose
propellers were mounted on shafts six or eight feet long
that protruded behind. There were floating markets in
the klongs that sold both goods and food. We were told
that at certain seasons the king's dragon-faced gilded
war canoes were brought out on the river in parade.

As the morning wore on, we tied up the boat and
stopped at one of the great temples that gleamed in the
sun with porcelain and gold. It was true porcelain, ex-
quisite china from a wrecked British warship, teacups
and dishes by the thousands set in cement to make sym-
metrical designs on the façade, walls, and roof.

We visited the temple of the Golden Buddha, a
newly discovered life-size image weighing five tons and
made of solid gold. For centuries it had lain in a junk
yard, its gold covered with plaster. The sawmill company that owned it finally prevailed on the monks of
Wat Traismitra to accept it. Two years later, during a
June monsoon, the storm cracked open the stone and the
monks saw the gold. It is believed that during the
sixteenth-century Burmese invasion of Thailand, the
golden image was coated to preserve the statue from the
invaders. Now it rested secure in its temple, its stern
and aquiline face gleaming in the candlelight, its ta-

pered and slendered waist quite unlike other represen-
tations of the prophet.

Jane went off to take pictures, and I sat with Sem
and told him of Jane's problem. "I want to take Jane to
the temple of the Emerald Buddha," he said. "she must
contemplate."

I was struck by the force of Sem's phrase. Contem-
plation was different from prayer. I knew prayer was
valuable, because in order to pray one had to formulate
in his mind what it was he was praying for. Con-
templation seemed an even more powerful word, for
here the force was directed not outward to a deity, but
inward, to accomplish an adjustment between one's self
and the universe.

"Things that come also can go," Sem said.

At the end of the morning, Sem led Jane and me
into the temple of the Emerald Buddha, the most sacred
spot in Siam. It stood in the midst of a shimmering complex of tiled, gold-roofed temples and shrines that surrounded the grand palace. In its vestibule was a little
altar where people were saying prayers. An old priest
was telling fortunes by shaking a set of sticks in a
cylindrical box. Sem gave Jane a coin for the fortune-
teller, and she pulled out the stick that was sticking up
highest in the box.

"What did you wish?" I asked her.

"Not much," she said quietly. "I don't want to make
it too hard for Buddha." That was all she would say.

Sem took off his shoes, and we followed the tradition. He led us into the sanctuary. High above, in the

candlelight of the altar, sat a child-sized figure cut from jasper, emitting a glowing radiance of green. Jane and I sat on the floor to contemplate the Emerald Buddha. Sem waited nearby.

It was very still in the temple. The light was dim. There was the faint smell of incense in the air. It would be easy, with the Buddha glowing there above, to listen to "the whispering of the dream." It would be good to have everything go on as today, with Jane beside me forever. But that would be asking too much of the Buddha. We were here to contemplate, not to pray.

10

THE VOICE OF
OUR ANCESTORS—
MATELA, 1962

I am a part of all that I have met.

—Tennyson's *Ulysses*

We checked our little red duffel bags through
to Crete and watched them disappear into the machinery of the Bangkok airport.

"We made it," Jane said. Then she slung her camera over her shoulder and headed for the gate.

After we had left Crete the summer before, the Professor, Elias Fassoulakis, had written to invite us to return and live in his house at Matela.

"I will have everything prepared for you," he
wrote. "We will listen to the voice of our ancestors and
hear once more their secrets from the depths of the centuries and the passage of time."

162